AGING

A Time for New Learning

David J. Maitland

John Knox Press
ATLANTA

Unless otherwise indicated, Scripture quotations are from the Revised Standard Version of the Holy Bible, copyright, 1946, 1952, and © 1971, 1973 by the Division of Christian Education, National Council of the Churches of Christ in the U.S.A., and used by permission.

Acknowledgment is made for permission to quote from the following sources:

To Beacon Press for use of material from Viktor E. Frankl, *Man's Search for Meaning*. Copyright 1968 by Beacon Press.

To The Christian Century Foundation for use of material from Richard E. Wentz, "Call Me Ishmael." Copyright 1980 Christian Century Foundation. Reprinted by permission from the 10/15/80 issue of *The Christian Century*.

To Adolf Guggenbühl-Craig for use of material from "Youth in Trouble and the Problem of Evil" in the *Andover Newton Quarterly* (January 1965).

To Harcourt Brace Jovanovich, Inc. for use of material from Anne Morrow Lindbergh, "The Journey Not the Arrival." Copyright © 1978 by Anne Morrow Lindbergh. Excerpted from a speech given by Anne Morrow Lindbergh at Smith College in August 1978, by permission of Anne Morrow Lindbergh and Harcourt Brace Jovanovich, Inc.

To the *Harvard Divinity Bulletin* for material from Margaret R. Miles, "Formation by Attraction: Vision and Responsibility." Reprinted by permission from *Harvard Divinity Bulletin* XIV/1 (1983–1984), p. 3 f.

To Henry Holt and Company from THE POETRY OF ROBERT FROST edited by Edward Connery Lathem. Copyright 1916, © 1969 by Holt, Rinehart and Winston. Copyright 1944 by Robert Frost. Reprinted by permission of Henry Holt and Company.

Library of Congress Cataloging-in-Publication Data

Maitland, David Johnston, 1922–
    Aging : a time for new learning.

        1. Aged—Religious life. I. Title.
    BV4580.M28   1987   248.8'5   86–46038
    ISBN 0-8042-1107-8 (pbk.)

        © copyright John Knox Press 1987
    10 9 8 7 6 5 4 3 2 1
    Printed in the United States of America
    John Knox Press
    Atlanta, Georgia 30365

In fond memory of JAMES W. GREEN, JR., 1885–1971
Loving father and father-in-law

Other books by David J. Maitland:

Against the Grain: Coming Through Mid-life Crisis
Looking Both Ways: A Theology for Mid-life

Preface

Around my sixtieth birthday I first began to wonder about the purpose of the last years of life. For the most part these stirrings were gentle. Eventually, however, my question was more insistent and more despairing: is it for nothing that we grow older? The end prospect was not imminent; my health was good; I was still capable of work I enjoyed; my important relationships were intact. There was no reason to believe that I could not continue to live with satisfaction. In large measure this has proven true. In health, meaningful activity, family, and friendships there is continuity between what I have been and what I presently am. My reflections have not been prodded by any dramatic departure from the familiar.

Still, something has changed. I cannot avoid asking myself what, if anything, should be different about the balance of my life. The fact that I ask the question is, I believe, not to be ignored. Something unfamiliar is stirring. Is it the distant but recurrent beat of some different drummer? It occurs to me that this unsought question of how to live my last years may be prompted by God. In fact, I have come to believe the question to be part of God's persistent effort to instruct me even as I age.

Such concerns about aging are symptomatic of what may be the greatest social change of recent decades. For the first time in human history a sizeable percentage of any generation, at least in the West but increasingly throughout the world, has the prospect of living to and beyond the Bible's promise of "threescore years and ten." This is a momentous phenomenon; never before have great masses of men and women had to come to terms with the issues of longevity. Until recently only the exceptional persons in any generation had to make sense out of their experience of far outliving their peers. The task of coming to terms with the later years is mine but hardly mine alone.

About a quarter-century ago, a family crisis crept quietly into my life in the form of a child's homework assignments. It was called "The New Math." Having to that point prided myself as a conscientious parent, encouraging an interest in education in our children both by example and exhortation, I suddenly found myself adrift in an uncharted sea. I had always been a good student of mathematics; in an instant, however, the help I had been able to provide an older child was next to valueless. "Our teacher doesn't allow us to do the problems *that* way, Dad!" was how my son reminded me that the times had changed. The skills which I had acquired at considerable cost were roughly as useful as a pre-Copernican understanding of the solar system. (That system is mathematically explainable on Ptolemy's assumption that the earth is its center, but the explanation is extremely cumbersome. Assuming the sun's centrality, Copernicus dramatically simplified the needed formulae. By a change of focus, such as is required as we grow older, he discovered both a truer and more beautiful orientation to our place in the cosmos.)

My deep conviction is that life's later years call for a new learning which is about as related to one's previous experience as was the new mathematics to the old or as was the Copernican to the Ptolemaic understanding. In aging one continues to deal with the same realities: my body is more or less what it once was, my relationships endure, my emotions are aroused or not by more or less the same stimuli—yet I find myself beginning to think about them somewhat differently. Without willing any change, I find that I do not see things in my seventh decade as I did earlier. Some new learning is being evoked.

As I resisted the New Math, and as the church rejected Galileo's theories, many of us are likely to resent the obligation to change as we grow older. Such resistance is understandable but must be overcome if we are to be able to see the opportunities of aging. New learning is required if we are truly to be our age and to be of any use to those who are younger. However, this learning need be neither instantaneous nor intimidating; if we are willing, growing older itself instructs us gradually. Because we all have come gradually to our present ways of thinking, particularly about ourselves—ways which need to be at least modified, if not discarded—it is important to realize that only by *gradual* increments will we be able to discover the delightful freedom of thinking in ways appropriate to our age.

Just as there are those who never discover that freedom as they grow older, there are also those who come to aging's wisdom while they are still young. Such people are rare, especially in this society; nevertheless, exceptional experience may have instructed them in ways which many of their elders resist. While such wisdom will probably never be widespread, it is important to emphasize that it may occur. This realization protects us against two erroneous attitudes: that only the elderly may become wise and that all elderly will do so. Regrettably, the latter is clearly not true. The former acknowledges that, while the wisdom is potential for all who age, it is not beyond the grasp of those much younger whom harsh experience so instructs.

The first step toward such freedom is to clear away the attitudes which blind us to what may be God's purposes in allowing us to age. There is a work of destruction to be done before any constructive approach to aging is possible. So deeply ingrained are the obstacles to such new learning that most older people either despair or settle for diversions which usually assure that they will never pursue the wisdom commensurate with their God-given aging humanity. It is this temptation to resignation that I would combat. To fail to respect its power is to assure failure in our undertaking. Both resignation and the temptation to underestimate its effects are formidable because, being inherent in so many of our ordinary attitudes, they are difficult for us to challenge. So much a part of normal adult life are they that we do not even readily recognize them or their possible need for modification. That an attitude or activity which has been functional for decades might become a burden, or at least less useful in one's later years, we cannot easily accept. As an established outlook changes, one begins to see some of the excitement and challenge of aging's new learning.

Of the many observations in the Bible about aging, I find one verse endlessly intriguing:

> So teach us to number our days
> that we may get a heart of wisdom. (Psalm 90:12)

While the poet's age is unknown there is evidence that he was no longer young. What is clear is the request for instruction—for a new learning—which, if followed, will yield a desired result. This ancient writer, whose tradition I take seriously, desired for his old age something which he called a wise heart.

What steps shall we take in order to gain a wise heart? How shall we discover what this new learning might be? Our first task is to be clearer than we ordinarily are about the ways of God's instruction. Chapter 1, drawing upon my experience over several decades as a college teacher, addresses this first step. Chapter 2 identifies several deeply held societal attitudes which can discourage aging's tasks. For example, there is virtually no encouragement to be intentional and positive about the realities of growing older. *Aging* is a dirty word. However, chapter 3 describes some experiential ingredients in the process of growing old which support the search for a wise heart. Chapter 4, "A Heart for Maintenance," suggests what may characterize such hard-won wisdom. The next two chapters look first at longevity's tutelage and then at the journey as a powerful image for one's coming to terms with the inescapable fact of aging. Finally, in chapter 7 I call attention to an added dimension of human lives before concluding with some remarks in chapter 8 about our need for usable images. As life, including a viable and often lovely environment, was provided for us, so we must help to provide for future generations. Christian life is not just a matter of self-cultivation. Jesus exhorts us to maintain the proper balance in our relationship to God, neighbor, and self, and this balance is no less important as one ages than it was in earlier decades.

A Native American observation may encourage some readers to dig further into this book: "When the student is ready the teacher will appear." Having long believed that we learn only what we need to know and being indebted to many instructors who came into my life at opportune times, I was not prepared for the quarter from which instruction comes in one's later years. *Aging itself will teach us but only if we are ready.*

As a person willing to learn and for those similarly motivated—or motivatable, I have written this book. The last word on aging is not here; it will never be written. In the meantime, however, thoughtful readers may better understand the heart of wisdom that God has in mind for those who are privileged to grow old.

While I am responsible for what appears in this book, it would be graceless not to acknowledge with gratitude improvements of the original manuscript which resulted from the professional attention given to it by Ginger Pyron and Joan Crawford of John Knox Press.

Contents

1

The Divine Pedagogy:
Abandoning Old Assumptions

All images derive from human experience. In metaphor or simile, and in visual images, we reason from what we know experientially to the less well known or to the unknown. We regularly use images, such as those of shepherd, artisan, or husband, in attempts to put into words our understanding of God.

Even more diverse symbols may be found in other than the Judeo-Christian traditions. Always and everywhere in image making, people draw on material, places, and events central to their lives. It could not be otherwise as they seek means to understand relationships between the varied aspects of their experience—both ordinary and extraordinary, between their lives and the vastly larger world of nature and other peoples in space and time.

Always the function of imagery is to assist people to make those connections which overcome the constant threat of isolation and its attendant loneliness. For good and ill, contemporary Western people have an ever-diminishing sense of these connections. Witness the much-publicized instances—such as that of Kitty Genovese of Queens—in which apartment dwellers watched but did nothing in response to a murder in progress outside their building. An effect of this erosion of the social fabric is that to the loneliness which many endure must be added the lack of connection with their own lives. We cannot make these inner connections by ourselves. This work requires other people and also images of shared humanity. As unique as each life may be, it is important to realize how much like all others we really are. Balancing these two ingredients of a life—one's distinctiveness and one's kinship with all others—is a difficult, endless, and crucial task. We need images which celebrate both our uniqueness as persons and our commonality.

In our search for such images, we especially need an image of God which can make us more willing and able to assent to the inevitability of aging. Our unavoidable progress through life's stages, including that of growing old, is God's precious gift to us. I am convinced that there are important things to be learned at all of life's stages, including the last. Comparatively few people are able to embrace this pedagogy; and I believe that this failure to live as fully as God apparently intended for us, especially during life's later years, results from the inadequacy of the imagery provided by both church and society.

A

We cannot escape the need for some image(s) of God, for only through imagery are our imaginations engaged. Only by means of images—God as Father or Mother, punitive judge, sacrificial lamb, maker of heaven and earth, or gentle shepherd—are we able gradually to be in touch with the vast range of our own complex lives. In our relationship to God we are free to be in touch with ourselves and to acknowledge our kinship with our neighbor. All other relationships, such as those of family and citizenship, free us to acknowledge only parts of who we are. In loving God we can acknowledge lovingly all that is true about us. And however broken we are, we can also acknowledge the oft-neglected coordinate of such love for God: love for self. In Jesus' summary of the law (Matt. 22:37ff.), the exhortation to love God, neighbor, and self assumes the inherent interconnectedness of the ingredients of our humanity.

Clearly, at different times and moods one image of God will serve us better than others: for example, the image of compassionate parent in time of loss or that of the stern judge in a period of rebellion. The key to the usefulness of any image is its ability, at a particular moment, to open us to aspects of ourselves which would otherwise be inaccessible. Lacking such imagery of God most of us settle for denying personal realities because we are unable to deal with them. More rarely the lid of Pandora's box springs open. In this instance a person can be overwhelmed by the uncontrollable emergence of masses of long-unacknowledged chaotic material.

Public worship—when some of the images of God are explicit in word, song, or rite—often evokes these extreme responses: either we deny personal realities, thereby concealing ourselves ever more completely, or we are moved to self-acquaintance in ways which deeply excite us. In worship we may actually find ourselves both stimulated and fearful in the realization that, beneath the veneer of order which we present to others, there is an inner life which is less controlled than we pretend. In mainline Protestant worship we are allowed only limited access to these hidden aspects of our God-givenness. Care is taken that nobody will be overwhelmed by the experience of the unconscious which the great images of God may evoke. On those occasions when I have attended a Black church service, however, I have met God at depths I rarely reach in more sedentary worship. Such services offer traditional but profoundly moving imagery; there I have opened myself to the sense of kinship across racial differences, the rhythmic persuasiveness of gospel music, the sensibilities resulting from centuries of enslavement, and the passion for freedom which often informs the sermon. In the presence of such images I find myself moved beyond my ordinary self-understanding to a feeling of oneness with all sorts and conditions of men and women.

Familiar images have an amazing power to deepen both one's sense of God's gracious presence and one's acquaintance with one's own inner life. Twenty years ago at an evening service of the Iona Community in an ancient abbey off the west coast of Scotland, I gathered with others for an observance of the Lord's Supper. I have never been quite the same person since. Sitting within walls at least fifteen hundred years old, I recalled with awe and a sense of kinship the generations of monks and others who had gathered similarly over the centuries. Particularly moving, however, was the unusual procedure for distribution of the communion bread. Each person in turn held the loaf before another and repeated the familiar eucharistic words "The body of Christ, broken for you." As I was thus served by my twelve-year-old son, again I was struck by the continuity of the generations, but this time I was open to the different ways in which the generations may relate. It is not always the older who convey the words of life. Through a novel setting and circumstance, a familiar image had taken me gracefully into the overlooked unfamiliar. I realized that not only am I father to this boy, I am also his child. Giving and receiving are mutual.

Such insights gained through the deep experience of inherited religious symbols reveal the profound differences between the imagery of religion and that of the advertising industry. In commercial images, no attempt is made to encourage deeper self-acquaintance. Instead, we are led to believe that our identity is wholly inadequate but that it will be appropriately enhanced when we acquire the touted product. The purpose of the advertiser's image is not to encourage reflection but to suggest a winsome substitute for that hard work. Even in an era which suggests often and in a variety of ways how eager people are to be in touch with themselves, the work of knowing and loving what one discovers about one's self is not inherently appealing. At the moment of self-recognition we are both attracted and repulsed. We prefer almost anything to this assignment, and the image-makers have taken full advantage of our aversion. They propose an easy, purchasable alternative for that work for which there is no substitute.

Religious images have exactly the opposite intent. Their purpose, by pointing toward that Ultimate Reality in and from whom we have our life, is to encourage greater truthfulness about ourselves. Such images invite what the image-makers suggest can be avoided. Where advertisements imply that value can be added to our lives by what we acquire, *religious images urge us to embrace the value of what we are and have been as the only route to what we may yet become.* Religious images urge us to recognize the good of which we are now capable, however limited it may be, rather than to conceal our abilities under the veneer of value ostensibly added by purchase. Through such images we can liberate whatever resources for good we actually possess—and these are greater than is ordinarily acknowledged—rather than inhibiting ourselves by accepting the implication that we are not worth much without possessing the advertised product. The intents of commercial advertisements and of religious images are radically at odds, and this is nowhere more evident than in their respective attitudes toward human potential.

These two kinds of images differ also in the depths of their rootage. Images fashioned for political candidates and consumer products often present a "magic" or effortless way to avoid fundamental work of human life-making by appearing to be superior to others. Usually the image-maker's appeal is to some transient anxiety within the society; a political image, for example, might appeal to the desire for a leader who is able to simplify both problems and resolutions in an age when issues are unavoidably complex. Images made for selling candidates intentionally obscure the tangled web of human history which refutes all such simplifications.

By contrast, religious imagery has its roots deep in the human past and has enabled generations of men and women to make some sense out of the best and worst of human experience. Inherent in the image of God as shepherd, for instance, is the realization that unguarded sheep are prey to predators. Without this reference to the perils of predation, the image of the good shepherd is merely sentimental. Religious imagery points a direction for possible resolution of real problems without minimizing the reality of the conflicts or suggesting that there is an easy way to have them disappear. Sheep will always need protection against predators. Tensions between races, sexes, ages, or ethnic groups—to say nothing of the fundamental conflict between the haves and the have-nots—will not simply vanish. The task for all persons is to be able to recognize the presence of these ambivalent ingredients *within* themselves: kinship and alienation, compassion and indifference, male and female, child and elder, poverty and riches, the entire rainbow of the races. As we become better acquainted with ourselves, we will grow towards the awareness that each particular person is all these things. In consequence we will act differently towards our neighbors, and they will know the difference. By our loving behavior they will be freer to be themselves with and for us. The God whose love frees us to be more fully ourselves, including in our aging years, works through our liberation to free others also.

B

The image of God as teacher is central to my thinking about aging as the final stage of human lives. Without always being able to identify precisely what the lessons are in each major era of life, I am convinced both that different things are to be learned in each and that ordinarily we are more able to learn those things then than at earlier or later times. The lures to such learning are both internal and external. Within ourselves, we may find a willingness to learn, a readiness to move on to the next stage of life and its lessons. Events outside ourselves, too—the accumulation of our experience—may make us teachable. The universal and poignant fact of mortality, for example, may fully sink in only after we are forced to come to terms with the reality of a friend's death. Just how we are able to deal with our unavoidable, often absurd experience is influenced greatly by our access to images. My own experience has persuaded me that the image of God as a very special kind of teacher can bring new awareness to help us uncover the agenda of life's last years.

In a disquieting period of mid-life trauma, during which I felt variously perplexed, alienated, weak, inadequate, and lonely, I gradually convinced myself that whatever was taking place within me was at least as much evidence of God's presence as of God's absence. The trauma was not just punishment for an ill-constructed life, though it was unavoidably partly that. My mistaken assumption was that only where and when I was in control was God possibly present. I was unable to acknowledge sadness, loneliness, fear, a sense of inadequacies, suspicions that I had made some unwise decisions, because these were at odds with the self-image which I had fashioned and which others reinforced. Little did I realize the mistake I had made in assuming that my ability to assure order may have been the best shield *against* God's presence. I felt more than a little liberated when I was finally able to admit my considerable imperfection. After an initial disorientation— my world had been turned upside down—I began to find possibilities for hope.

Had this been the whole story I would probably not be writing fifteen years later. Fortunately, it was not. Aided by Augustine and by many more contemporary writers, I came to believe that in addition to receiving some deserved punishment, I was in my troubled condition being called to something. Probably the turning point came when I sensed God's exhortation as well as judgment. Something might yet be made of my flawed life. Like Jesse Jackson's borrowed comment at the Democratic National Convention in 1984, my thoughts were apologetic but nonetheless hopeful: "God has not finished with me yet!"

I came to sense the presence of the Divine Teacher who had been in my life since its inception. Amidst all of the seemingly contrary indications to which I, like all people, had been subject, God was continually present, urging me to grow toward that humanity appropriate to men and women made *imago dei*. However, in order to be open to God's life-giving but noncoercive presence in my life I had to assume responsibility for that life. Flawed it clearly was; others may have contributed heavily to its making, but it *was* mine. The first and only question, once I had admitted that I was none other than this, was to wonder what good might be made of it—not necessarily the good which I might intend, which is endlessly infused with self-interest, but the good which God might accomplish once I admitted the flaws. In this moment I realized that I had but limited ability to control the *consequences* of my attitudes and behavior. Some say that animals instinctively sense things about us and act accordingly. Persons suffering certain forms of mental illness are also said to be especially perceptive of attitudes of which we may not be aware. Perhaps small children, and certainly the aged, are sensitive to being patronized—especially when we are unaware of the attitude. With our limitations and such strengths as we have, we are what we are; and we have some potential for moving with the tutelage of the Divine Teacher. However in bondage we may be to destructive and self-destructive attitudes and behaviors, there is no human life from which the image of God has been wholly expunged.

We are never abandoned by God; the God-given desire to be more in touch with ourselves never ceases. This I take to be evidence of that self-love to which Jesus exhorts us, and consciously or not, it also expresses love for God who has so fashioned human lives. I further assume that such honest self-love is the only reliable basis for the neighbor-love to which Jesus also exhorts us. We can love each other only when we know how much like each other we are. These loves for self and others are possible, I believe, only when we acknowledge God's presence amidst the flaws in us all. Before God we are acceptable, as Cromwell graphically expressed it, "warts and all." How we *feel* about ourselves as we actually are—an admixture of potential for both good and evil—determines utterly how we relate to ourselves and the world.

What I came to see in this process of self-acquaintance, during which my understanding of God underwent a sea change, is that God has implanted in us some sense of the direction in which lives made in God's image should mature. The image has not been obliterated and experience may help us to recognize it. There is no assurance that we will so use our freedom; the evidence to the contrary is often seemingly overwhelming. But the lure of a deeper, more connected, loving life is ineradicable in every person. That we are shot through with contradictions is not the last word; that we may die—and probably will—without having been able much to resolve them is also true but not decisive. What matters, and only this, is the direction in which, in our better moments, we *want* our lives to move. Out of that desire for greater honesty of self-presentation, greater openness to the diversity of lives, greater willingness to relax the desire to control outcomes, God will accomplish some good. This is but to recognize the most radical message of the New Testament: we are justified by grace. We do not control but we may be agents of some good if, by being willing to be who we are, we are able to recognize gladly that God has had the first and will have the last word.

But it is not an overriding word, for God is not a coercive teacher. The Divine Pedagogue beckons us towards learning and teaches us—if we are open—through our own imaginations.

C

As I tried to discover new directions for both my personal and professional life, changes gradually took place in my work as a college teacher. In general they represent my efforts to translate into the classroom some of the consequences of the self-understanding to which I was coming. By a step-by-step evolution rather than by any dramatic change, I tried to follow the inner leadings of the Divine Pedagogue.

The first step was to recognize that as a teacher I had modeled my behavior on those from whom I had learned. Virtually all of the many courses I had taken in college, seminary, and graduate schools had proceeded as lectures, and I had reams of class notes to prove it. What did not occur to me for more than a decade was the assumptions about learning which underlay this method. While searching through the multitudinous course lectures which I had on file for some particular reference, I came across a folder of notes for a class I absolutely could not remember having taken. The writing was clearly mine and the teacher had enjoyed a good reputation as a lecturer, but it was as though I had never been there. Professorial lectures, I concluded, are a most effective way often to assure that little or no learning occurs.

My reaction may have been extreme, as many of my colleagues continue to insist. Nor was it ever congenial to all students. For the former it threatens the basis of their authority: demonstrably superior competence about matters which the lecturer controls. For the latter it suggests responsibility for their own education. I was questioning the adequacy of an educational theory which benefits those who are attentive, can write quickly, and are able to give back a decent version of what is fed them in lectures. To my emerging understanding, something crucial was being omitted in this popular procedure. Many students, perhaps sensing that nothing really important happens in the academic classroom, select courses on the basis of the entertainment value of the teacher: how able is this professor to keep my interest in a topic that really matters little to me? The opportunity for education is short-circuited when all or most of the burden for making material "interesting" rests on the teacher.

It is wholly appropriate to expect a teacher to be interested in his or her subject. However, I am convinced that if the right approach can be found, every subject of study is potentially electrifying. Everything in the world of nature and of human experience is capable of arousing the student's imagination. By such imaginative connection with any given body of material the student as a learning *person* is drawn into the process. As a person whose God-givenness includes intellect and a wide range of sensibilities, each student possesses resources for recognizing the bearing of any academic topic on his or her life and for developing a point of view toward it. There are a wide variety of perspectives on any reality, and the proper work of higher education is to create an environment in which those perspectives may engage each other in the interest of a more comprehensive understanding of the complex reality being studied. In this process the teacher will always have the advantage of superior knowledge, but it is not sufficient—indeed, it may well be injurious—for nothing but the teacher's knowledge to be displayed. The task of academic authority is not to overwhelm others with one's erudition but to create an environment in which students recognize their inescapable role in the learning process, gain confidence in their contributions, and develop an appreciative sensitivity to the contributions of others. With this new understanding, I discovered that, as a teacher, I was more interested in the *process* of learning than in its product-content. Once the imagination had been engaged and the student had begun to experience both adequacy and present limits, I was confident in his or her ability to acquire whatever content material was needed. The opposite approach had provided me no such continuing assurance.

Three powerful assumptions about teaching and learning arose from my discoveries: (1) The responsibility for determining the syllabus and the ground rules of the class rests with the teacher and thereby acknowledges the teacher's distinctive training and experience. Occasionally, brief lectures may be needed, but they are kept at a minimum. (2) The responsibility for being interesting is shared; the assigned texts and students' responses to them are at least as integral to the learning process as the special competencies of the teacher. The absence of such pyrotechnics as the dazzling lecture creates the opportunity for students to discover the anguish and the genuine excitement of shared academic work for which all have done private preparation. (3) Most importantly, in such an environment students realize clearly that nobody can *give* them an education. Learning is a painful but potentially exhilarating process in which competence and character combine: one can experience the courage to risk expressing an interpretation, the courtesy of initially suspending disbelief with reference to another's views, the tenacity to grapple long with an assignment, the capacity for dialogue in working through conflicting interpretations. In the last analysis I suspect that such qualities determine one's competence. For as long as we have *human beings who learn*—who have varying capacities for risk-taking, for holding together seemingly contradictory evidence, for acknowledging the impossibility of absolute truth—we have unending but varied resources for learning. Liberal learning always involves *persons* and is committed to their maturation as persons of character.

Faith mandates inventiveness. Belief in the living God endlessly calls us to see something more in every situation, from a mid-life trauma to a class assignment, than was visible yesterday. I came to see more about my life as a teacher than I had earlier been able to imagine, and I have tried in the classroom to encourage such inventiveness in students. I force my views on nobody, just as the Pedagogue has never insisted that I learn only God's ways. What I sense to be true to my experience, however, is that God's inner tutelage persists throughout one's life and that accumulated experience may make us more amenable to learning. This, I am convinced, endures into the final years of every life; and I believe that many would be so instructible if they had adequate access to the image of God as such a distinctive teacher. God's respect for us as pupils—some more willfully resistant to instruction than others—endures to the end.

God's presence in human lives is, in part, to be seen in our varied capabilities of mind and imagination, and in our capacity for taking ourselves and others seriously. I emphasize this because so often these gifts, which surely can be and are misused, are said to be inherently wayward. This judgment I reject. Furthermore, however thoroughly we may have misused our God-given capabilities, the God-implanted desire for their proper use is never wholly obliterated. The right teacher at the right time can awaken within us the desire to move in a direction more consonant with the awareness of ourselves as made in God's image.

Few more powerful illustrations of the dramatic onset of self-discovery exist than that which occurs to King Lear in one of Shake-speare's greatest plays. Lear's insight into his sins of omission occurs in the midst of two violent storms: thunder and lightning and driving rain to terrify the homeless king, and the threat of inner madness which he has long dreaded. Only by this combination of attacks from without and within are his eyes opened to something important which, as a once all-powerful chief, he has failed to do. Gifted at playing the polit-ical games which lead to success, he has been insensitive to the fate of the least of his subjects. Only upon discovering that he has been out-witted by daughters who have professed to love him, only when he has been brought as low as his lowliest subjects, only after he has been driven mad by recognizing the folly of his prideful rejection of the only daughter who truly loves him, is he able to see the inadequacy of the leadership he once provided. His epiphany is almost too late, but not quite! Lear finally sees that it is not enough to be powerful and clever, to be a successful manipulator. During his rule people depended on his concern for them; he betrayed them in his zeal for monarchical games. Lear's realization finally dawns: "O! I have ta'en/Too little care of this" (*King Lear*, III, iv, 32–33). The once great manipulator is at the point of becoming a wise and chastened old man.

It may well take some such traumatic unsettling of one's estab-lished order and reputation to arouse that willingness to make us able to recognize the diminished, long-neglected evidence of God's presence in one's life. Because the onset of aging is a somewhat gradual experi-ence rather than a dramatically instructive one, it is imperative to be able to affirm it as another of God's peculiar opportunities for learning. I am increasingly convinced that, given our ability to admit its onset, the experience of growing older may be the most instructive era of a person's life.

2

Aging:
Inhibiting Attitudes,
Subtle Resources

Reasons are numerous for reluctance to recognize one's later years as potentially highly instructive. In our society, which attaches great importance to formal education, one of these is the assumption that learning occurs only in the classroom. This preoccupation with formal schooling is disastrous to our ability to learn from our experience. What is of value for aging is simply the material of our life. The aged must learn to value their own experiences as the primary source of understanding appropriate to their last years. In this totality lie the significant threads of each person's distinctive story; and this story, however modest, is what we each need to become better acquainted with as we grow older. It is not the achievements of exceptional people, often much older than we, about whom we need to learn. Because of the contrast between such lives and our own, such information may only inhibit our hesitant steps toward self-acquaintance.

A

Many obvious facts, such as progressive frailty and retirement, contribute to a negative attitude toward aging. Persons lacking physical health and persons no longer employed violate two powerful values in our society: the importance of being independent and of having a job. However, even more insidious are those assumptions that less directly undermine the worth of the aging person. Four such merit attention: the importance of control, the possibility for initiative, the appropriateness of prevailing media images, and the insistence on answers. While these assumptions may be at least as harmful as constructive at all stages of life, they are especially damaging to people trying to recognize and to undertake the work of the later years. To the extent that they cannot be shaken there is no hope of purposefully affirming one's aging.

1

Many Americans hold tenaciously that it is crucial to have both the control of one's present life and the confidence of control in one's future. We carefully plan our schedules, enroll in programs to maintain health, make retirement plans, set up schemes for financing children's education. Unfortunately, however, there is no way to assure that the control will be effective. Recently, for example, I learned of the death on the tennis court of a man in his mid-fifties who had long been dedicated to health maintenance. His attempts to control his body's health were both thorough and excellent; what was not controllable, though, was his genetic inheritance which made the heart attack more likely. Similarly, there are innumerable people who, often with little or no warning, are stricken with nonlethal ailments to which they must adjust for the rest of their lives. Every day we read of unanticipated events by which "the best laid plans of mice and men," as Robert Burns observed, "gang aft a-gley" ("To a Mouse," *The Poetical Works of Robert Burns* [Glasgow: David Bryce and Son, n.d.]). Overwhelming evidence shows the impossibility of maintaining such control as many of us seek.

Furthermore, a dangerous amount of willpower is required to maintain the amount of control to which the most compulsive aspire. These people are determined that nothing will keep them from their immediate plans. At this very moment, in the midst of the second major winter storm in five days, the interstate roads here are littered with the cars and trucks of men and women whose willfulness far exceeded their ability to accept any limits. The costs of such determination to be in control are unfortunately not limited to highway accidents. At a more subtle level all the personal relationships of such willful persons have been shaped and misshaped by longtime involvement in patterns of control. Such an environment extinguishes the more natural give-and-take, lubricated by lots of humor, by which less determined people deal with life's frailties and limits.

2

Cousin to this desire to control is the assumption that the capacity for initiative is limitless. Certainly, some people are capable of seemingly boundless initiative. I recall my virtual disbelief several years ago when I saw my first one-legged skier. Having trouble negotiating the slope with two skis, I was properly amazed at his skill on one. Today we have Olympics for the handicapped. This is nothing but admirable and has occurred only because some people took the initiative of which others deemed them incapable. Change comes when some take a lead of which others could not even dream. As movements by Blacks, women, and the aged have demonstrated in the past generation, this same phenomenon is true in political and social areas. It would be evil to try to confine human initiative in any specific way.

Yet there are limits. Failure to acknowledge this has been the cause of much unnecessary anguish. If the aging are unable to relinquish some of this assumption of limitless initiative they will be unable to get on with what may be their proper business. Clearly, these matters are tricky, since the very ability to recognize aging's agenda requires an initiative which is able to challenge prevailing attitudes towards growing old.

What we ignore, however, is the despair that results when our great expectations collapse. Our assumptions about boundless possibilities are often quite punitive when they focus, as they usually do, on individual lives. Persons nurtured on the assumption that initiative is limitless are easily discouraged when they discover otherwise; consequently, many people are unable to value the modest changes that may be possible when opportunities are much reduced. The pendulum swings 180 degrees from limitless optimism to the bleakest hopelessness. Tiny accomplishments, which are within the capability of anyone with only occasional moments of consciousness, may appear pathetically insignificant.

Studies of the rapidly vanishing peasant societies reveal dynamics dramatically opposite our own. In part because they are much more directly connected to the natural world, these societies begin by recognizing life's contingencies. In their experience nobody is exempt from uncertainty; the lives of all are admittedly much more dependent on uncontrollable forces than we incline to think any life needs to be. Paradoxically, from their realism about inevitability emerges the capacity for initiative. Unburdened by great expectations, they are able to seize and value the occasional modest opportunity for achievement which comes their way. Especially for the aging there is wisdom in the peasant outlook which needs at least to be balanced with the prevailing assumptions about initiative's limitlessness. The experience of limits is one of the mounting realizations of life's later years. Given this inevitability, one needs resources, often unneeded earlier, which will guard against despair and unnecessary passivity. Nothing else will enable aging men and women to value the foreseeably diminishing initiative of which they will be capable. In one's advanced years the tasks that one undertakes and must learn to value will not be those which one once undertook. They will be appropriate to such realities as diminished energy. Only a badly misguided society will fail to honor them.

3

In large measure it is to such a society that we belong. We value but one of the stages of life through which all who reach the age of retirement have passed. We call it "adulthood" and it holds the assumptions that total control is both possible and desirable and that opportunities for initiative are limitless. Daily reinforcement of the desirability of such adulthood comes to us through the media. Aspirations are determined: how we should appear, what we should have and desire, what we should avoid. The images in the commercial media are anything but subtle.

Whereas the text usually at least implies that the product is for everyone, that it will enhance all lives, the visual images are rarely other than slender, prosperous, youthful-appearing, white Anglo-Saxon men and women. The image which all are urged to desire is in fact impossible for most viewers to embody. While this may have little adverse effect upon the purchases of the advertised products, it has a devastating effect upon those who have no possibilities of themselves possessing the traits of the images on the screen. To be either fat, poor, old, nonwhite—or, God help you! some combination of these—is to be of no value in this society. The imaging to which we are daily exposed marginalizes, isolates, and destroys hope in millions of people. Among those so affected are the aged who, at least in many homes, spend unconscionable hours sitting before a box which anesthetizes as it diminishes. Eventually, the bondage to hopelessness can be total.

4

The final assumption which erodes the desire to work at the agenda of one's later years is the assumption that there are answers to all questions. Undergirded by the need to be in control, by the belief that initiative is boundless, and by daily bombardment with the media's reminders of the acceptable way to be, to look, to act, we are impatient when confronted by unanswered questions. They imply an impotence which we abhor. In large part we respond to such restlessness by concentrating our attention on questions to which answers can be found. These tend to be quantitative and easily within the capability of a society of engineers. The current fascination with computers may be the clearest evidence of the effort to assign exclusive importance to answerable questions.

The problem, especially as one ages, is that such information is decreasingly useful. At some point in the lives of most people quite different questions begin to emerge: What is the meaning of life? On what bases have I done what I have? Neglected what I have? To what kind of a society have I contributed? What useful thing have I done for anybody? Am I satisfied with the quality of my relationships? Have I been neglectful of my inner life? What inner life do I actually have? Why am I often overcome with regrets? Have I understood well enough the involvement of my life with people far removed and often unknown? Have I paid proper attention to the extent to which my life has been determined? Have I let myself be deceived about the extent I have been in control? Have I possibly proceeded on a cluster of assumptions which were never as adequate as I and others pretended? Why have I been plagued with resentment toward others? Have I faced the fact of my own mortality? Is there time to get in touch with the realities rather than the pretenses of my life? If so, am I motivated to do so? These are like the questions which Paul Gauguin, at an early age, asked himself before abandoning his bourgeois life for Tahiti: "Whence come we? What are we? Whither go we?" Few will react as dramatically as he; few escape the questions. John Steinbeck put the questions yet another way: "Have I lived enough? Have I loved enough?"

To such questions there are no easy answers. That is part of what keeps many from recognizing their importance. Behind this fact, however, is the societal aversion to the unanswerable. We are ill prepared to live with these questions, and our avoidance of them is especially punishing for the aged. Two responses are commonplace: either denial of the questions in a continuing pretense that they have not yet surfaced; or deepening depression both with the questions themselves and with one's inability to embrace and be nurtured by them. I would not undervalue either the reality of the questions or the real difficulty in knowing how to respond to them. Probably most older people have found themselves so confronted. The point is to emphasize the nonproductive anguish caused to older people by societal attitudes which are negative both to the aging and to the kinds of questions that age often generates.

To recognize that there are some things that one can do is clearly a central ingredient in all human experience. It may be as simple as being able to swallow some water from a glass held by a nurse. However, in the course of growing older there are often even harder things to swallow, such as those unanswerable questions which people wish we would not ask. This is the double bind: being unable to suppress those questions appropriate to one's age, questions in which others are usually not interested. How better to assure isolation and uncertainty? Whereas youth may break out of a similar impasse by taking on the frenzied activity of adulthood, this is no longer an option for those whose active years are past.

B

The widely held attitudes which discourage older people from searching out and working at the agenda appropriate to their stage of life are enduringly powerful. They do not cease to exercise control over us simply because we can intellectually identify them. They have been too long intrinsic to our self-understanding to be so easily overcome. Paradoxically, however, many helpful resources lie hidden within these negative outlooks.

In my experience it has long been evident that there are no unchanging answers to the sorts of questions we have been asking. At every stage of life some of these questions are asked and answered. Part of the work of aging is to recognize how one has been answering basic questions, how one has actually made choices and invested energy. That the process of self-recognition often begins earlier may well explain why life's middle years are so traumatic for many. We are able finally to recognize patterns of preference in our lives and to face their undeniable consequences.

At some point most people discover that they have lived out the advice given by Rilke to the young poet who pleaded for answers:

> . . . try to love the *questions themselves* . . . [answers] cannot be given you because you would not be able to live them. And the point is to live everything. *Live* the questions now. Perhaps you will then gradually, without noticing it, live along some distant day into the answer.
>
> (Rainer Maria Rilke, *Letters to a Young Poet*, trans. M. D. Herter Norton [New York: Norton and Co., Inc., 1954] 35)

Whether or not we like the answer we find at the "distant day," and what to do if we do not like it, is part of the burden which age must learn to carry.

The realization that there are patterns of preference in our lives and that they might be discernible occurred to me recently in a very homely way. Upon slipping into a pair of our grown son's shoes, I noticed that my son and I walk differently. That we do not wear our heels down identically made the shoes, which were my size, quickly uncomfortable. Our different gaits would not be apparent to the untrained eye; had his shoes been new I would not have noticed anything.

It takes time and usage for a pair of shoes to register the user's way. Similarly, our lives record consequences of our many choices. How we have chosen to invest ourselves or to withhold from involvement may not be inferred from a single episode or even a cluster of them. Over time, however, one acts as one is. Aging enables us to begin to identify these patterns of preference. To quote another poem of Burns, aging gives us the gift "to see oursels as ithers see us!" The gains foreseen by the poet could be vast:

It wad frae monie a blunder free us,
    An' foolish notion:
What airs in dress an' gait wad lea'e us
    An' ev'n devotion!

("To a Louse," *The Complete Poetical Works of Robert Burns*)

Oscar Wilde's *The Picture of Dorian Gray* tells a story of the unavoidable inner changes that occurred over the years in a man who gave free rein to his desires. As Dorian Gray followed his preferences, consistently making self-indulgent responses to the questions that arose in his life, his secret self-portrait—concealed from all eyes but his own—recorded his steady, horrifying deterioration. That Gray finally took his life illustrates the despair to which some people may be driven by the discovery of their life's actual patterns—and those patterns' undeniable consequences.

Certainly, not all the discoveries of the later years may be depressing ones. In the language of Erik Erikson some older lives are possessed by despair and self-disgust, but others are marked by integrity (Erik Erikson, *The Life Cycle Completed* [New York and London: W. W. Norton and Co., 1982]). Many aging persons discover beauty and connectedness which, because of their modesty, they may not have recognized earlier. These are men and women who have long been quietly centering their lives; by valuing their own incompleteness, they have acted on an acknowledged and treasured relationship with people and with the natural world.

Most lives fall into neither extreme. When self-recognition becomes possible most of us discover both elements of integrity and grounds for despair. This is the starting point for aging's agenda: recognition of the accumulated evidence of one's life. To admit the evidence, however, does not assure willingness to undertake the task of growth. That willingness will itself be the consequence of whatever prior risky personal growth one has ventured. We are dealing here with a kind of iron law; courage and faintheartedness breed their kind. Much as we might wish otherwise, we are confronted by one of the hardest truths of the New Testament: "For to [those] who [have] will more be given; and from [those] who [have] not, even what [they have] will be taken away" (Mark 4:25).

Several years ago, almost by chance, I found myself in the midst of an instructive correspondence with three elderly men. None knew the others, nor that I was exchanging letters with them; only one did I ever meet personally. His was a lively and growing mind, a firm but generous spirit. He was what I call a life-giver, and for several years we exchanged stimulating material. The second man was embittered, quick to criticize, and always suspicious that some advantage was being taken of him. Unable to encourage or even to enjoy, he was a life-denier. The third I knew least, mainly by others' reports. He was secretive and erratic, moving without apparent cause from euphoria to despondency. Perhaps he was a life-avoider. These three men did not develop these qualities in their old age. While there may have been some exaggeration of traits as they aged, it was clear to me that they were as elders what they had been as boys and younger men. The first man asked hard questions over the entire course of his life and lived his way into a series of consonant answers. The second apparently insisted that the answers at which he had arrived early in his life had to be made to fit whatever questions were posed by later times and circumstances. The third man may have had questions, but he was as opaque about these as about any answers he may have found.

1

One of the tasks of growing old is to recognize one's actual answers to difficult questions, answers which have gradually evolved from the responses to a myriad of less important questions. What one will be able to do with this knowledge will be determined both by the character of these deep answers and by the images to which one has been exposed. Often unconsciously, one's deep answers are influenced by the images prevalent in everyday living. To the extent that our sense of our own humanity has been largely shaped by the images which television projects, we are ill equipped. As suggested earlier, the visions constantly offered are too limited to be useful to our humanization. Not only do they pander to our inclination to feel good about ourselves only as we are successful consumers of products; much more seriously, they impair our ability to connect positively with our own lives. If the only desirable visual images of humanity are young, slim, prosperous, white Anglo-Saxons—and if we are none of these—on what basis are we able to affirm our own lives? How are we to avoid feeling marginalized, isolated, and progressively hopeless?

The greatness of a society ultimately is determined by the adequacy of the images to which its people have ready and repeated access. It is this which makes the arts important: by their images we are able to assent to the realities of our own inner lives—their depths and heights—and thereby to recognize gladly our relationship with all other life. Inasmuch as our lives are grounded in adequate images and as we are able regularly to renew their acquaintance, we will not be marginalized, isolated, or deprived of hope. We will all remain different, since we each are one of a kind, but this will be a means to solitude rather than loneliness. We will always resist absorption into a faceless mass—for example, of "wretched old people in nursing homes"—because we know our kinship with all sorts and conditions of people. We will know despair, but it will be in tandem with deeply grounded reasons for hope. Our lives reflect the adequacy of the images by which we have been nurtured and to which we continue to have access. The availability of such images, at least in memory, is crucial to people who are struggling with the question as to whether it is for something or nothing that they age. By the images to which we have been meaningfully exposed during our lives, we answer the deep questions which eventually give our lives their particular shape. In many instances what is deemed good or ill fortune reflects nothing other than the adequacy of the images which we have internalized.

That this is not a matter of the amount of one's education or of extended travel was first suggested to me through a short article written twenty years ago. Reflecting on the problems of wayward youth and an understanding of evil, a Swiss psychiatrist wrote as follows:

> Parents who are able to give their children a spiritual framework in addition to external forms are promoting their ability to deal with evil and the devil later. This framework may be oriented religiously, ethically, or even aesthetically. It has nothing to do with going to concerts, reading best-sellers, possessing encyclopedic knowledge, or achieving the highest academic degrees. It only means that there is a certain endeavor to understand the world in a deeper sense and to organize life according to this understanding, perhaps through a religious, ethical, or aesthetic approach. In this way a poor hard-working Sicilian farmer, who has only one year of schooling but who is very concerned with the Catholic religion, praying with his children every night and trying to teach them the doctrine of the church as far as he understands it, has more culture, more symbols ready for his children's use than, let us say, a highly paid executive who works very hard and attends a concert from time to time, but who has never tried to understand the world in a spiritual way.
>
> (Adolf Guggenbühl-Craig, "Youth in Trouble and the Problem of Evil," *Andover Newton Quarterly* [January 1965] 25–6)

The adequacy of the images which one has to work with in age or adolescence, or at any point between, is not determined by the numbers of galleries one has visited. Everything depends on how integral to one's self-understanding and ways of responding to experience some simple images have been.

Yet in my experience certain travels have been important. I will never forget being taken by a Black friend to see one of the few pieces of sculpture in our national capital honoring a Negro. As we stood in a somewhat shabby park in the presence of an image of Mary McLeod Bethune I understood for the first time something of the importance of "Black is beautiful!" to millions of men and women marginalized for so much of our common history, including that day's television. My eyes were opened to my own guilt and to the nobility of so many previously invisible people. Of the myriad images in the many galleries in Washington, was any as important as that of Mary Bethune? Not on that day for me, surely; nor on other days for many who, as I now realize, are truly my brothers and sisters.

In a small city in France I encountered another image which changed my life. Part of a triptych by Matthias Grünewald, it depicts such a crucified Christ as I had never seen. Influenced previously by largely sentimental, so-called religious art, I was initially repulsed by the wounded, diseased depiction in greens and yellows. Yet I was fascinated also, partly by the attention being directed to the figure by the pointing finger of John the Baptist. My eyes were opened when I learned that it had been prepared originally for a hospital, a place to which came those hopelessly marginalized and isolated by illness. Here was a welcome to which they could respond, a source of hope in one who was in all ways like themselves. Here was an image which enabled some, in their brokenness, to believe that wholeness was recoverable. They could find courage for their faintheartedness. I can imagine many saying with Paul that, because of this image, whether they lived or died they did so in the Lord. They no longer felt alone, and this is the precondition of all health. Whatever the outcome of their treatment, they were helped by Grünewald's imagery of the Messiah to know with the psalmist that God was indeed the Lord of the generations of the well and the sick. Without making light of the isolating effect of all illness, this Isenheim Altarpiece reminded me powerfully of the continuity both of human suffering and of God's compassion. Because of my comparative good fortune I cannot be too often recalled to these enduring realities. Suffering is an inescapable component of human experience, but, graciously, it need not be the last word.

From France I traveled to Norway where quite to my surprise I encountered another series of images from which I hope never to recover. As must have been true of Grünewald's Altarpiece, I was unknowingly ready for Gustav Vigeland's disclosures about human experience. While much more is imaged in the almost two hundred figures—from small bronze bas-reliefs to larger-than-life stone pieces—I was grasped by his acknowledgment of the ambivalence which characterizes life at all stages. By his powerful and often tender depiction of men and women and children in varying degrees of relationship and isolation, by the intimacy and alienation of his various images, I began to be able to assent to conditions of my own life which I had long thought it necessary to deny to myself and to conceal from others. Viable I knew I was; broken I could not admit. Perhaps it was part of Vigeland's gift to me to be able to admit that, like those sixteenth-century men and women who found welcome at Isenheim, I too needed to be received so that I might receive myself. Though these two artists are long dead, I live with and by the images given to me by a late medieval German painter and a turbulent modern Norwegian sculptor.

The importance of the available images in the society into which we are born cannot be overstressed. They are crucial for all people but especially for the aging who must undertake work which is little encouraged when not actually discouraged. Theirs is a necessary twofold work: of self-acquaintance and, often with limited contact with others, of understanding that they do belong to some reality larger than themselves. Great images are vital to our self-understanding, and perhaps it is *only* in aging that we become able to appreciate them.

A few years ago a professor of historical theology at Harvard Divinity School contrasted our modern perspective with the outlook of simpler, earlier people. I report her observation as an act of nostalgia for a world I never knew and as a plea for its recovery:

> Interpretation of the visual imagery, available to all the members of a society on a daily basis, involves nothing less than the willingness to entertain the perspective of human beings who did not think of themselves as primarily constituted by a reasoning faculty, ego, or subjective consciousness, but by their connectedness to the natural world and the human community through notoriously fragile bodies. To begin to see what they saw in the images that surrounded them in their local churches, we need to recognize that it is possible to lead a life of amazing beauty and richness that understands itself as grounded in physical existence and its exigencies, from this foundation gathering visual symbols that articulate, actualize, and enhance the life of the body. This does not imply a life that is either limited to biological functions or one that is focussed on these functions. From a primary identification with the life of the body, one can extrapolate a world of relationships that receive their origin, their structure, and their energy from physical existence—kinship, social relationships, and the "body politic." Attitudes, values, and concepts can also be based on physical existence; Christianity itself can be understood not primarily as a nexus of ideas, but as concrete participation in a body—the "body of Christ"—in which

human life is understood as given in physical existence (creation) and con-
summated only in physical existence (resurrection of the body).

(Margaret R. Miles, "Formation by Attraction: Vision and Responsibility," *Harvard Divinity Bulletin* [October-November 1983] 3–4)

These are our ancient cousins who would have been fed by Grünewald
and perhaps even by Vigeland. Despite great adversity they would have
known that it is for something that we grow older.

2

In my earlier discussion of initiative and control I may have given
the impression of their irrelevance to one's later years. That was certainly not my intent; varying amounts of both endure in most lives to
the point of death. Having recently visited a hospitalized person with
but a few hours to live—a person who had for some weeks essentially
"given up"—I know that, while capable of very little initiative, she
continued to exercise some control. As she lost interest in my presence
it was not only fatigue which closed her eyes. In his important early
book, initially titled *From Death-Camp to Existentialism*, Viktor
Frankl rightly insisted that we retain control *from within* to the very
end. Writing of his experiences as a survivor of German death camps
during World War II, Frankl states that it was not the adversity of conditions per se which killed many prisoners. People died not as a result
of the unbelievably inhumane treatment but when they lost the will to
live:

In spite of all the enforced physical and mental primitiveness of the life in a
concentration camp, it was possible for spiritual life to deepen. Sensitive
people . . . were able to retreat from their terrible surroundings to a life of
inner riches and spiritual freedom. Only in this way can one explain the
apparent paradox that some prisoners of a less hardy make-up often seemed
to survive camp life better than did those of a robust nature. . . .

Everything can be taken from a man but one thing: the last of the human
freedoms—to choose one's attitude in any given set of circumstances, to
choose one's own way. . . . Even though conditions such as lack of sleep,
insufficient food and various mental stresses may suggest that the inmates
were bound to react in certain ways, in the final analysis it becomes clear
that the sort of person the prisoner became was the result of an inner deci-
sion, and not the result of camp influences alone. Fundamentally, there-

fore, any man can, even under such circumstances, decide what shall become of him—mentally and spiritually. He may retain his human dignity even in a concentration camp.

(Viktor E. Frankl, *Man's Search for Meaning: An Introduction to Logo Therapy* [Boston: Beacon Press, 1967] 56–7 and 104-5).

Although control and initiative are inflated by contemporary over-emphasis, they remain desirable abilities. The point is simply that, because there will be some diminution of both control and initiative as one ages, our attitude toward their role must be modified. Some things may be relinquished. Clearly, it is impossible to define how much of either trait any individual will or should assume. No two persons will be capable of identical degrees of control or initiative, nor should they be so urged.

Futhermore, the purposes of control and initiative may change as one grows old. In late adolescence and during the long years of adulthood both control and initiative are functional in pursuit of success. This goal determines the qualifications and experiences to be sought, the status and roles to be gained, the reputation to be earned. One is unlikely to be deemed successful without considerable initiative and a good deal of consistent control. Lack of such qualities in those decades is predictive of what the world calls failure.

Aging persons, noticing their diminishing initiative and control, may feel a sense of personal failure, not realizing that few if any of those who hard and long pursued success feel otherwise. It is critical at this point to recognize that the achievement of success is not fully within any individual's power. "Success" is determined by the judgment of others. In the pursuit of it I am not the absolute master of my fate. My chances of being favorably judged will be increased by ample initiative and control, but those things cannot assure it. Innumerable factors—some whimsical, like one's performances on psychological tests as a basis of promotions, and others arbitrary, like prejudice toward one's sex, race, or age—will determine the level of success which an individual may achieve.

Dissatisfaction with life so understood can gradually open one's eyes to the inadequacy of success as a goal of life. In addition to recognizing the roles of whimsy and arbitrariness, and the impossibility of being successful wholly on one's own, the aging person realizes that there is ever less time left for living. "Have I lived enough?" and "Have I loved enough?" are the existential questions which the active pursuit of success requires one to suppress. Such questions are from God who apparently intends some different things for our later years than from the earlier decades of life. For all things there is a season. At age fifty, one more clearly understands the psalmist's wisdom; our days *are* numbered, and this fact often prompts us to wonder about the life we may have lost in living. In their later years many people come to find Thoreau's question suddenly germane:

> Why should we be in such desperate haste to succeed . . . ? If a man does not keep pace with his companions, perhaps it is because he hears a different drummer. Let him step to the music which he hears, however measured or far away.
>
> (Henry David Thoreau, *Walden* [New York: E. P. Dutton, 1941] 237)

Here is a great verbal image for the aging: to move to a distant, different rhythm. It suggests folk music with people coming together and needing each other for the sake of the dance, rather than an isolating disco beat that calls attention to the self. Anne Morrow Lindbergh, speaking on the occasion of her fiftieth college reunion, has put succinctly the change in outlook which is especially apt at this point:

> . . . when I was young I felt more solitary and special. I thought I was different from everyone else. Now I have learned how similar our experiences are under our different disguises—how alike we are under our differences. Now I am old, I feel less isolated and more compassionate; less critical and more sympathetic. . . .
>
> (Copyright © 1978 by Anne Morrow Lindbergh. Excerpted from a speech given by Anne Morrow Lindbergh at Smith College in August, 1978 by permission of Anne Morrow Lindbergh and Harcourt Brace Jovanovich, Inc.)

In aging one is searching for the alternative to the pursuit of success. We search for fulfillment, for a way of being ourselves independent of the judgments of others. This is what is distinctive about fulfillment: knowledge of it is only from within. The irony is that the initiative which contributed to one's success does not readily transfer to the search for fulfillment. Adulthood's initiative is directed to self-justification, but the initiative of one's later years involves a twofold willingness: to acknowledge how much one's success was not earned, and to allow one simply to be one's self. At this point we are on the very edge of religious language.

3

Before turning to these matters, however, we should note the often inherent loneliness of the work of the later years. An individual needs heroic initiative to live against the grain, but most people need also some support from others in their desire to be somewhat different. Obtaining such support may be difficult in a society which absolutizes success. It requires small communities of encouragement, which is part of the vocation of church and synagogue. Those who are growing older need an environment where they can confidently explore the work of aging.

It is unfortunate to have to use the word *work* for this undertaking. I do so in the sense that the person in therapy must work at self-acquaintance. This is not something that anybody else can do for us, though the more skilled the therapist the better able the client will be to accomplish his or her individual work. The point is that all persons have their own distinctive network of resources and resistance. No two persons "recover" in quite the same way or to the same degree, but all may be helped to draw upon their capabilities. Something similar is true for all people as they age.

The tasks of growing older parallel a theory first voiced by Richard Cabot over seventy years ago (Richard Cabot, *What Men Live By* [Boston: Houghton Mifflin Co., 1914]). This Boston physician suggested that there are four basic ingredients in a human life: work, play, love, and worship. Each person must learn to balance them properly. In our society, work tends to outweigh the others. It is from the dominance of work, which we might understand as activity directed towards the pursuit of success, which the aging need to free themselves. This suggestion does not urge complete inactivity; however, it insists upon a different focus for one's activity, one which enlarges the roles of play, love, and worship.

What needs to be brought under control is the imperiousness of adulthood's work mania. Rather than excessive enthusiasm for one aspect of life, we need a loving and deliberate attention to those neglected aspects of the self which Cabot identifies. Perhaps, ultimately, we require not a new kind of control but less worry about controlling. In the words of the title of one of the last Beatles songs, we are called to "Let It Be." Let there be more ample place in aging lives—though not in those alone!— for play, love, and worship. By these means may flower, for the enrichment of all, aspects of our God-given being which work mania could never evoke. By these means, finally, one may gain a wise heart.

3

Wise Hearts:
Assenting to Ambiguities

As we ask ourselves what characterizes a wise heart, we must be quite clear about two matters: deeply held, largely unexamined, *attitudes* hearten or dishearten our ordinary days; and while changes in these attitudes are possible, such changes will be gradual and are never free of cost. In the course of aging we are being weaned away from attitudes which have been functional, or so we have believed, during the productive decades. As we grow older we are being called beyond productivity as the basis of self-understanding. Or to put that positively, we have in the later years opportunity for a quite different kind of productivity. If adulthood primarily focuses on external accomplishments and acquisitions, the new direction will be primarily inward and evaluative.

It is a slight change in one's "heading" that principally characterizes an emerging wise heart. As in sailing, a subtle change in the heading will in time bring one onto a different, perhaps smoother or more
appropriate, path of direction. Being able to assent to aging's change of
heading is crucial. As one ages, death is clearly the destination; nothing
will change that. I want, however, to suggest how we might make
slight changes—how we might follow a more appropriate course—so
as to move in that direction in the liveliest, most fulfilling, most comprehensive way. The external achievements that have absorbed so
much energy and attention during young adulthood and the middle
years are decidedly less valid for those whose time left is much less
than the time they have already lived. Activities such as producing, acquiring, and consuming, though perfectly appropriate for younger persons and never wholly abandonable, have two adverse consequences
for the aging who insist on maintaining these things' centrality: they
discourage attention to one's inner life, and they provide a decreasingly
relevant basis for self-understanding.

Erik Erikson suggests that a person's final task in life is to assure
that a sense of integrity prevails over the temptation of despair. Reasons for feeling disgust with one's life are always present; these will
not be obliterated by pursuing *external* activities. Such activity simply
does not allow one to deal with the universal and particular sources of
despair. We remain faulted creatures to the end. We must be able to
affirm this fact while recognizing that the acknowledgment of our own
frailty is the key to such integrity as is allowed to God's creatures.

Through faith in God the aging have the means for assenting with
integrity to the enduring incompleteness and isolation of lives. Freed to
pursue such wisdom, they may be a source of blessing to themselves
and to those who are younger. These older and wiser hearts, without
having lost all interest or competence in external matters, will be able
to put such activities in their place, as the young are rarely able to do;
the gracefully aging are aware of something better—because more appropriate—for their important later years. Such awareness is the gradual consequence of attention to one's long-neglected inner life and to
the answers at which one has, often unknowingly, arrived.

A

Rilke's prediction to the young poet was true: with the passage of time we discover that answers *have* taken shape to life's hard questions. To such questions one does not simply think out the answers, at one long sitting if necessary. Rather, by cumulative decisions—which were informed by subtle values often unrecognized at the time—one becomes a certain kind of person. A man or a woman emerges from this gradual process with distinctive answers. At no earlier time might sufficient evidence have accumulated to enable one to see oneself with the clarity which age makes possible. One has become a living answer to previously imponderable questions. Some older persons have all the beauty of the wise heart for which the psalmist prayed; others, like Dorian Gray, are disgusting because filled with self-disgust.

Most people will discover themselves to be somewhere between these extremes. Like a character in a recent novel, we find that we need courage to assent to the lives which we have actually led. Reflecting on an evening in Palermo with his mistress and recalling his wife's hysteria in response to this action, a prince remembers—in an Augustinian way—two lines of a poem he chanced upon in an earlier, similar circumstance:

> . . . *donnez-moi la force et le courage*
> *de contempler mon coeur et mon corps sans dégoût.*

(Giuseppe di Lampedusa, *The Leopard*, trans. Archibald Colquhoun [New York: Pantheon, 1960] 38)

This fiction is all too real for most people in the course of discovering their answers.

Even those with the wisest hearts are not wholly free from regrets. Most discover eventually that they have not been as adequate a spouse or parent, employee or employer, citizen or person of faith as they might have liked to be. All wind up wishing that in certain circumstances they had been less fussy or less passive, more assertive or more consistently cooperative. Perfectly to balance these basic ingredients and to employ them appropriately in life's varied circumstances is impossible. Over the decades and through innumerable minor decisions we have become too much of one thing, too little of the other. Had we been less obtuse at any particular time we might have sensed negative reactions and made minor changes which would have resulted eventually in a somewhat different older person. The fact is that all are, in varying ways and for somewhat different reasons, obtuse—and since obtuse, in some degree blind. To move in the direction of wiser hearts we must first open our eyes to what has been and, because of that past, what now is. This is the first and the inescapable price to be paid for the psalmist's wisdom.

Since this task involves the exposure of personal failures (sins of commission) and of undeserved but presumed privilege (sins of omission), it is not surprising that some persons reject the poet's pursuit. It is easier by far, and always involves a shred of truth, to be resigned to the answers one finds: "It was all predetermined. I never had a chance to be other than I am." However, it is a small step from such resignation to smug self-satisfaction, closely akin to the spiritually lethal trait of self-righteousness. From this there is little hope of escape, because clarity of self-perception is precluded. Clearly, grave perils are inseparable from the discovery of the answers which are one's life: despair and self-justification are the extremes. Common as both may be, they destroy the possibility of that growth which may be distinctive to the later years. Despair destroys hope, thereby binding initiative; self-satisfaction denies need for hope, thereby trying to maintain the old controls in a new day. Both lack any transcendent understanding of the self's origin beyond time or of the comprehensive network of life's relationships. Despair and self-satisfaction are equally dead ends: they ignore the endless God-given potential for becoming other than who one presently is.

The alternative to the defeatism of both despair and arrogance is the discovery of justification by grace. By paradoxical acknowledgment that one both is and is not responsible for one's life-answers, one can be both truthful and hopeful. In the last analysis each person can share the far-reaching truths of the psalmist's realization: life neither began with me nor will end with me. Long before my birth there was God, the Lord of all the generations. My life was not created *de novo*, without blemish or limitations. The world into which I was born, and which has continued to shape me, was partly centered in God and constantly tempted to other loyalties. To such a world—partly caring, partly care-less; partly compassionate, partly indifferent; partly brave, partly timid; partly base, partly noble; partly daring, partly cautious—I have always belonged. This is central to the answers I have found; I cannot deny or obscure such reality. It both could not have been otherwise *and* is of my making. Often unwittingly, but always unerringly, I made the mul-tiple small choices which eventually yielded my life-answers. I both knew and did not quite know what I was doing.

Amid the confusion and multiplicity of our choices, we often *do* know what we are doing, and we pretend more than we realize. For what we know and pretend, we do not deserve mercy. It is this fact which makes so radically liberating the fundamental assurance of the Christian gospel: "While we were yet sinners [so knowing and so pre-tentious] Christ died for us" (Rom. 5:8). Or, as Paul concludes one of the most compelling reassurances of the divine mercy: ". . . [nothing] will be able to separate us from the love of God in Christ Jesus our Lord" (Rom. 8:39). Ultimately, whatever our success or failures, our reasons for arrogance or despair, it is not by these that we are justified or condemned. We are the children of God, as have been all preceding generations and all that will follow. It is almost too much to believe, except as we are led beyond the misguidance of self-disgust or self-infatuation. Both misguide because they have not learned that ulti-mately all is of God who is the Lord of all generations.

In this realization that, though we often have not recognized it, our entire life has been God's gracious gift, we have the firm ground on which to come to terms with the answers we have discovered about ourselves. We find reason for regret and contrition rather than for resig-nation or self-disgust; we find reason for modest expectation of change rather than for hopelessness. Although we may not become signifi-cantly different, what we *are* is only the potentially fruitful beginning point. The radically new consideration is what we will *do* differently. As one justified by grace, I know how much like all other people I am. My pretense of uniqueness in my earlier years is an illusion I relinquish in favor of this acknowledged kinship. No longer do I wonder how I can make my neighbors serve my interest; instead, I am now free to be aware of my neighbors' interests and to discover how even I might serve them.

My world has been radically changed, turned inside out, by the acceptance of God's grace. Not only may I be truthful about myself without despair, but I may acknowledge kinship without fear of being diminished by it. This transformation will not happen overnight. Like all good things, it will occur gradually as I make the myriad little choices of my late years—choices which will yield yet more vital and comprehensive answer in whatever time remains. There are no instant or easy panaceas. The point of discovering the answers at which one has arrived is not thereafter to sit on them. Rather, in one's later years, these answers become the basis of somewhat different and, I believe, even more important questions.

Before turning to these questions I want to conclude the present discussion with a story which illustrates the possibility for change and the enduring continuities of life.

Three days after Christmas, 1984, a man was buried at the Arlington National Cemetery. (This story was reported on "All Things Considered," National Public Radio, 28 December 1984, and in *The Washington Post* on that same day.) Jesse Carpenter's funeral was but one of a dozen there that day. One of Washington's street people, he would hardly seem to have warranted wide news coverage. That there was more to his life than a passerby might have noticed before his death accounts both for the media reports and for my inclusion of them here. His final behavior illustrates the continuity of lives despite dramatic change of external circumstances.

Jesse Carpenter died in Lafayette Square, just across the street from the White House, as a result of exposure to extremely cold weather. He might have sought shelter that night but for the fact that his wheelchair-bound friend of twenty years, who survived the freezing temperatures out of doors, abhorred shelters. They all lacked means of access for the handicapped, and he hated the embarrassment of being carried in. Some men might have abandoned their companion under such circumstances, but not one who received the Bronze Star for exceptional bravery under conditions of great risk during World War II. Jesse Carpenter had been so honored in 1944 for carrying wounded comrades to safety in the midst of heavy enemy shelling. Unmindful of danger, he was a caring, risk-taking friend both on the battlefield and in life's unheralded winter nights.

Needless to say, Jesse Carpenter had not gone directly from demobilization to the streets. After the war he had married, fathered children, and apparently settled into a middle-class existence. In 1962, however, he walked away from that family to pick up life on the streets. This combination of factors—extreme youthful heroism, abandonment of a lifestyle widely honored, decades of survival characterized by the loyalty which eventually caused his death—warranted the news coverage. I include the story here as a vivid reminder that, while lives may change in apparently significant ways, who we are in the depth of our concern for and commitment to others endures. At a point in his post-war life Jesse Carpenter discovered some things about himself and acted on this knowledge. He may have regretted his unfitness for domestic life and the hurt which his departure caused. He had reason for contrition. Nor was his life after 1962 trouble-free, for he was several times admitted to veterans' hospitals for injuries received on the streets. But he acted from integrity in the last deed of his life, a deed which was both continuous with and at odds with parts of his past.

B

Gaston Bachelard, a modern French philosopher, offers some intriguing, suggestive insights that explore the connections between youth and age, age and images:

Great images have both a history and a prehistory; they are always a blend of memory and legend, with the result that we never experience an image directly. Indeed, every great image has an unfathomable oneiric [dreamlike] depth to which the personal past adds special color. Consequently, *it is not until late in life that we really revere an image, when we discover that its roots plunge well beyond the history that is fixed in our memories.* In the realm of absolute imagination, we remain young late in life. But we must lose our earthly Paradise in order actually to live in it, to experience it in the reality of its images, in the absolute sublimation that transcends all passion. A poet meditating upon the life of a great poet . . . wrote: "Alas! we have to grow old to conquer youth, to free it from its fetters and live according to its original impulse." . . .

Poetry . . . *offers us images as we should have imagined them during the "original impulse" of youth. Primal images, simple engravings are but so many invitations to start imagining again.* They give us back areas of being . . . *and we have the impression that, by living in such images as these, in images that are as stabilizing as these are, we could start a new life, a life that would be our own, that would belong to us in our very depths.*

(Gaston Bachelard, *The Poetics of Space*, trans. Maria Jolas [New York: Viking Penguin, 1964] 33 [italics added])

Here is a most promising secular understanding of the vocation of aging. Bachelard suggests an utterly positive vision: "we could start a new life . . . that would belong to us in our very depths." Few have voiced such important hope for the late years. Furthermore Bachelard relates the possibility of an utterly new life to one's earlier decades. This connection of age and youth particularly appeals to me, for it presents an image far removed from Shakespeare's description of life's final phase as "second childishness and mere oblivion."

Youth and age have many things in common. Both tend to lack money and power; both are restricted in sexual expression; both are out of the mainstream, often excluded from certain public places (in number they make adults nervous); both have high chemical dependency, though to different "pushers"; both have high suicide rates. Most important for our immediate purposes, the fact is that both stand at thresholds about which they are uncertain. Told by many that they are going to love life beyond the threshold, both the young and the old are understandably not sure. In adolescence and in advanced age, men and women are about to give up some known freedoms, pleasures, and obligations for some very uncertain new ones. They find themselves in a situation requiring wise hearts. The two groups are equally unable to number their days, but youth will resolve its dilemmas quite differently from those who know that they have already lived the great majority of their years. The young and the old will cross their respective thresholds but in different ways and for different reasons.

Of the many desires of youth, none may be more important than the double yearning for wholeness and for honesty. Energy it has in abundance; the problem is how to deploy it in ways which take account of youth's myriad impulses. How is a young person to relate burning passion and social compassion? How, at a level urgent for many students, to integrate mathematical and verbal skills? How to do justice both to the need for solitude and the need to belong? These ambivalences, which are present in all lives, are for adolescents the source of both heightened excitement and comparable frustration. It is never readily clear how the inescapable parts are to be related to each other. Certainly this wholeness is rarely achieved when one is young.

The common, and probably unavoidable, way to resolve the adolescent tensions is what I call "adulthood." Out of youth's chaos most people achieve some order: a career is chosen, a partner selected, and some values recognized. The process is almost universal. Perhaps because of its commonality the price of this simplification is less frequently acknowledged. The yearning for comprehensiveness has been tucked away wherever it could be concealed, into or under job and family and allegiances. For a long time, for most people, the accommodation works. In the preoccupations of adulthood—of establishing oneself, of learning to be a spouse and a parent, of giving time to community responsibilities—much can be ignored temporarily. But for reasons which often arise in mid-life from an unsettling of the achieved order, some yearnings of one's youth cannot be indefinitely ignored. In the midst of the very busyness of so much adult life, a frenzy which is itself supposed to indicate that all is well, emerge questions which suggest otherwise. These arise from the initial lack of clarity about values, self-awareness, and one's motivations for a choice of both mate and career. That these unavoidable deficiencies have consequences explains mid-life's traumas.

The other important characteristic of youth is its desire for honesty, especially about one's self. So extreme is this desire, and so lacking are young persons in an informed perspective, that some are pathologically self-critical. Usually the passion for truthfulness gives way to the apparent adequacy of adulthood's roles for self-preservation. Too often and too easily, one becomes nothing more than the lawyer a client sees, the doctor a patient depends upon, the parent one's own children know, the minister a congregation expects. Fortunately, there is much more to any one of us than these roles encompass. Truthfulness about this "much more" begins to seek expression during the middle years, and if the process is not blocked then, it may come to fruition late in life. Is it not truthfulness rather than pretense which is the source of beauty and goodness? Is it not ever more accurate self-awareness which enables us to escape the confines of even the best of roles? We have always been more than meets the eye, more even than we can remember.

These two distinctive characteristics of youth—the desire for wholeness and truthfulness—are shared by the aging. After the lack of self-awareness and the pretenses of adulthood, the resurgence of these desires should be heartening to the aging and can be nourishing to all ages if we as a society can put aside our fear of integrity and candor. Adulthood's roots are often shallow, but in maturity they can be both deep and strong.

If we are fortunate, late in life we discover *from our experience* that we do revere an image whose "roots plunge well beyond the history that is fixed in our memories." The wholeness and connection for which youth yearns are intrinsic to our being. We are not isolated integers, separate from the rest of life. We belong both to our contemporaries and to all life that has gone before and will follow us. A traditional hymn succinctly characterizes the vitality of such awareness:

> Standing in the living present,
> Memory and hope between,
> Lord, we would with deep thanksgiving
> Praise Thee most for things unseen.

> (W. P. Merrill, "Not Alone for Mighty Empire," *The Pilgrim Hymnal* [Boston: The Pilgrim Press, 1958]; permission by the estate of William Pierson Merrill)

These "unseen" fundamental relationships to past and future, so long denied or at least unacknowledged, may become in aging both visible and precious.

Nor are we the self-made, and therefore judgmental and isolated, men and women we have long pretended. For so much of whatever we have become we are indebted to innumerable mentors, who in a host of ways helped us to become what we are. That we do not make ourselves is one of those great images whose roots plunge well beyond personal memories. This is part of what we affirm by acknowledging God as the Lord of all generations: that people have endlessly been providing for each other environments in which human potential might flourish rather than be blighted. In a brilliant, brief introduction to the study of religion, Richard Wentz supports and extends this point:

> The "other" is always present to me, by way of the other individual, the other family, the other color, the other group, the other nation. I must respond to that which is the "not me," yet which by its presence is already part of me. To the extent that I am appreciatively aware of the presence of

the "other" in my encounter—to that extent will I respond creatively and not in defensive hostility.

Now it seems to me that this level of the encounter with otherness is just as formative of the religious mind and religious traditions as is the more awesome encounter with the *Wholly* Other. Any encounter with otherness is the encounter of a "more than" in our midst.

(Richard E. Wentz, "Call Me Ishmael," *The Christian Century*, 15 October 1980, 968)

Is it not some such awareness of connection and interdependence that informs the opening lines of Psalm 90? However tempted at other times to think only of his individual life, in composition the psalmist knew that life to be simply one strand of a fabric woven and being woven through all generations by that God who is from everlasting to everlasting. This awareness combats the threat of ultimate oblivion: it is the knot by which the psalmist's particular strand of life is held within the vastly larger and more complex tapestry of all lives. In no way has his life been diminished by the acknowledgment that that God is also the God of his fathers and children. His personal wholeness contributes to and is itself enhanced by the wholeness of the human generations under God. He has been enriched in the only way that is assuredly enduring: he belongs! From such a God he has reason to believe that there is yet a wise heart to be received, providing that he can learn to number his days.

I recently received a letter from a college friend who is recovering from a "mild heart attack." In reflecting on the effects of this experience he spoke of a sense of personal mortality which had not previously mattered much to him. He has always known, of course, that one day he would die. Intellectually we all realize that Ponce de Leon's search is doomed. In the past two months, however, he has realized existentially that death is always just a heartbeat away. Unlike his earlier letters, this most recent letter to me contained warm expressions of affection and also a lament over the superficial, privatized conversation characteristic of his social life. I take these to be evidences of a man in the process of gaining a wise heart: given the need to number his days, he now knows and can express the fact that he cares about such things as his long-term friendships and the future of the world. In remarking on his social group's indifference to such perils as the arms race, saber rattling foreign policies, and environmental pollution, he has manifested a markedly more urgent concern for future generations.

The psalmist was urging us to do something more than simply pay attention to the time we may have left to live. Learning to number our days also involves learning to value the myriad offerings in each day's experience. Rather than numbly, blithely, or hurriedly moving through our hours, we need to attend to them: to notice wherein they may be life-giving or life-denying, to be grateful for opportunities gained and repentant of those missed. Clearly, such ability to pay closer attention to one's own days is rarely possible during adulthood's breathless years. Then there are deadlines to meet, certifications to earn, car pools to chauffeur, bills to pay, promotions to seek, property to maintain, and so forth—all that Zorba described as "the full catastrophe!" It may be unavoidable that these adult years will be busy decades; the tragedy is that we have been led to believe that to be frenzied is to be fully alive, that the preoccupied heart is the wise heart.

In the prologue to the Fourth Gospel John makes momentous statements about the incarnate Logos. One sentence is especially relevant here: "He was in the world, and the world was made through him, yet the world knew him not" (John 1:10). John, of course, is speaking of the world's inability to recognize the Word of God incarnate in Jesus as the Christ. Similarly, however, in the course of assenting to our adult roles we often lose sight of the great images which should inform our self-understanding. We come to think of ourselves as self-made, as not needing others and having no responsibility for them, as being unconnected to the past and having little care for the future. All of these attitudes are false, but we attempt to live as though they are true. Made in God's image, we nevertheless try to stuff ourselves into smaller, more manipulable images of the human. At least for those years of pretense we often act as though we did not know to whom we belong.

If we are lucky—and luck might include a "mild heart attack"—something will intervene to arrest us. If we are lucky we will become aware of some revered image deeper than life-as-rush-and-acquisition. By entertaining a less frenzied image we might just be able to start a new life "that would be our own, that would belong to us in our very depths" I emphasize again, however, that older people are not sentenced to be passive and inactive, negatively rejecting the compulsive busyness of earlier years. Two of the happiest and most vigorous married couples I know, all four now in their eighties, are reasonably typical illustrations to the contrary. The approach of their later years certainly did nothing to remove these persons from the mainstream of living and loving. One couple were in their sixties before they met, fell in love, and married for the first time; the others lost spouses at about age seventy and met and married thereafter. All four have more of the delightful qualities of youth than have many people half their ages. The movement I urge is wholly positive: one can choose to be active or not, affirming or rejecting activities for what are increasingly one's own reasons.

Nor is this to urge self-preoccupation, which is antithetical to the new vision of one's kinship with others. Other people will continue to have claims upon our time and energy, but we will be available to them for reasons arising from our very depths rather than merely from a sense of duty or the obligations of a role. Our motivations will be more from the heart, because we will be wiser about ourselves.

During the last week of the year I often read at least the conclusion of W. H. Auden's Christmas oratorio, "For the Time Being." In these lines the poet reflects on the post-holiday letdown that many people experience. Having been in the presence of a great image, having felt briefly the wondrous gift and blessing inherent in the birth of the Christ, we must return to the everyday world. Nothing seems quite as bright as it may have earlier in the month; there is almost constant temptation towards despair or passive resignation. The contrast between the glory of the seasonal vision and one's daily chores may seem intolerable. But if we are fortunate we will have seen that the image of God incarnate is not simply an annual opportunity for euphoric diversion. The vision is for the sake of the present. As Auden says, it is the time being which is to be redeemed from insignificance. Yesterday's bills have to be paid, today's lessons have to be learned, tomorrow's world must be kept from destruction. The great images of the Bible are never ends in themselves, never treasures to be locked away for occasional private delight. They are for the sake of the dingy, daily world— that it may become less so. Those who have seen the Child, however dimly and from a distance, are so inclined. By taking in this great image, or being taken by it, our hearts are wiser than they could otherwise

be: we know that we belong, that we both have and have not made ourselves, that—thank God!—our "roots plunge well beyond the history
that is fixed in our memories."

C

The losses of control in aging are real; we need not minimize that
fact. One's body will be frailer; one will lose the freedom to abandon
situations with which one has become dissatisfied; one will have more
difficulty making new friends; one will likely have less income in retirement and possibly greater expenses. The task at this point is
straightforward and difficult: a shift in values is required. We must
come to see that the controls we desired or pretended when we were
younger were perhaps less valid objectives than we believed and that
they probably decrease in validity as time passes. There is, for example, no fountain of youth in which our bodies may be made young
again. We can be profoundly grateful for surgeries and medication
whereby some parts of us are repaired or replaced and the deterioration
of others is arrested. But we will not regain all earlier physical controls
by some bionic leap. Nor will any of the other losses mentioned above
be recovered. Two facts, however, ameliorate these losses: an aging
person will have some diminution of interest in the kind of control he
or she once deemed critical, and new areas exist in which gentle initiative may be increasingly rewarding.

Gradually accumulated experience over the years often helps to diminish one's earlier interest in total control. Some of this experience
reminds us of limitations we once either could or thought we could ignore. For example, I was once able to enter a season of downhill skiing
without preparation. My legs were strong enough to handle those demands. Some years ago it became apparent that if I intended such seasonally strenuous activity, I had to begin to get ready soon after Labor
Day! By lifting weights for a couple of months before the first snowfall
I have been able to continue to enjoy this sport. Gradually, however, I
have had an increased interest in cross-country skiing, an activity
which I can do more easily and safely. Eventually, as I notice my
changing limits, I may relinquish both these sports. I will, as it were,
gradually and willingly give up that which will be taken away from me.

In other and more immediate ways, too, experience instructs us. Being able to travel extensively, which was once highly stimulating, now interests me less than it did. I realize the superficiality of much of my travel: a year after a trip, and certainly a decade after, I recall very little of a journey that required considerable effort and expense. Am I better off having seen and forgotten the flora and fauna of England, Greece, or Mexico or being currently enchanted by the birds and flowers of southern Minnesota? Without having lost all interest in travel, I nevertheless know that I am fully stimulated by my appreciation of those parts of the universe immediately at hand. With Lao Tsu I find much of compelling interest constantly close by. The natural history in my own backyard changes endlessly; my long-term relationships have many more facets to explore than I realized; in my smaller world I have no lack of opportunities to discover and observe the wonders of creation.

In this context I am reminded of Darwin's seventeenth- and eighteenth-century English precursors, such as John Ray, Francis Willoughby, and Gilbert White, who devoted their attention to careful local observations. White, for example, never gathered information more than a few miles from the parish he served; and his observations of the cricket, which remain definitive, were confined to those few crickets he watched in the church burial ground. Why have we come to believe that to discover anything important we must travel far and wide? Do we thereby become less parochial? Do we become wiser? And perhaps more importantly, what do we lose in the frenzy of our pace? During the television broadcast of *Nicholas Nickleby* I was struck by an episode involving the Brothers Cheeryble and their old, beloved employee, Tim. Rejecting the brothers' plans for his gradual retirement, which included his removal to a peaceful place in the country, Tim emphatically stated his preference for familiar surroundings:

"There an't such a square as this, in the world. . . . Not one. For business or pleasure, in summer time or winter—I don't care which—there's nothing like it. There's not such a spring in England as the pump under the archway. There's not such a view in England as the view out of my window. . . I have slept in that room . . . for four-and-forty year; and if it wasn't inconvenient, and didn't interfere with business, I should request leave to die there."

(Charles Dickens, *The Life and Adventures of Nicholas Nickleby* [New York: New American Library, 1981] 454)

Like the reduced desire for wide horizons, one's need for money is also less imperious in age. The urge to acquire things diminishes once closets are full of rarely used clothing and shelves are lined with unread books. Time for reading and reflection becomes increasingly precious under the tutelage of gradual experience; consequently, the lure of new acquisitions subsides. As a teacher of mine once observed, aging is a time of simplification. We come to have our own reasons for letting go of things we have long clutched avidly; and despite some recurring sadness, the gradual pace of this process gives us time to relinquish our hold gently. Thus freed from unnecessary trappings, we can discover the beautiful and vital new insights which I believe God has reserved for the later years.

The wisdom of aging has the potential to change all of our relationships with the external world. It is an exploration of inner space to which we are invited as we grow older. As we proceed in self-acquaintance we become somebody different: we become truly familiar with who we are. This, I believe, is the key to the beauty of some old people. They are in touch with the central sinews of their own story, and we enjoy and admire their self-connectedness, their absence of pretense. In the presence of such men and women we are more able to be ourselves. What an invaluable gift older people have to give to others! By their familiarity and lack of embarrassment with themselves, we are freed from the need to engage in the profitless pretense characteristic of so much social life. Embodying Buber's "I" and thereby unafraid of being diminished by invidious comparisons or competition, older persons can provide the environment in which the rest of us know that we too—for all our imperfection—are simply, and wonderfully, persons. As physical life ebbs, one can become a true life-giver. The spark—the spirit of the living God, if you will—is passed on. The continuity of the generations, of whom God is indeed the Lord, is assured by the gifts of the aging.

As one relinquishes control over those areas of life that interfere with such beautiful self-acquaintance, one can simultaneously begin to exercise new, gentler controls that are appropriate to the growing wisdom of age. Rush must be avoided, regular time to be alone must be sought rather than abhorred, and—most importantly—receptivity must replace manipulation. Fortunately, as one ages, rush becomes ever more difficult. Initially, of course, most of us who have led rushed lives react to our new slowness with resentment, if not disbelief. The first time one is breathless upon taking a familiar staircase two or more steps at a time, the first recognition that the symptoms of a routine cold linger weeks longer than they once did are potentially dismaying evidence that the era of rush is coming to an end. However, if we are lucky the folly of our earlier frenzied living may dawn on us, and we will begin to discover some of the things we have been missing. Some of these will be beautiful and nourishing, others ugly and challenging. Both begin to reach us as we change from the speed and remoteness of air travel, or even of ground transportation, to walking or strolling. Much feeds the mind and challenges the imagination on an ordinary trek through the woods or along a city street. Only as our pace of life decreases do such realities have access to us; only without rush are we capable of being lovingly attentive to whatever is nearby.

Once freed from the wheels of rush, which always involves agendas and priorities largely determined by others, we are able to take time to be by ourselves. Initially this too may be a bewildering experience for those whose previous activities have been largely not self-determined and whose time alone has been filled with distractions. With less rush, however, one may come to choose rather than to avoid time alone. This may not be easy; indeed, to *will* rather than to tolerate such time by and for oneself may be for many older people their most difficult task. In a recent public television program an older woman, advocating unconditional patriotism, contemptuously dismissed the importance of self-nurture: "Love of self is boring!" (Gary Gilson, "Night Times," KTCA–TV, 15 December 1983). Leisurely self-acquaintance, of which frenzied lives have so little, may elicit any emotion from contempt to pleasant surprise, but surely, if attentively exercised, it will not result in boredom.

Finally, an important function of those who are slowed down and willing to be alone is to begin to substitute receptivity for manipulation. Possibly fatigue assists this change, though clearly it does not assure it. The belief, for example, that self-acquaintance is boring shuts off the primary source from which we might begin to receive input. Messages from within, primarily memories and the colors with which they are tinged; and impressions from without, such as the flicker of a bird's wing, the winter sound of last summer's residual leaves in the hard maple tree, the evening news from some troubled overseas capital—these are the sources to which we can attune ourselves. Promptings from the unconscious and reports from the world can be God's means of access to us once we cease controlling and begin to listen. We speak less when older not because we have less to say but because we have heard ourselves *ad nauseum* and because there is much that we are just beginning to learn. As a long-retired friend recently wrote to me, "There's so much to enjoy where I once didn't know anything was!"

I mentioned earlier that the areas for new initiative as one ages become increasingly internal. This is the case both because one's former abilities for external controls diminish and because one's attention is drawn elsewhere. The need for such a shift of focus is inherently spiritual, though the initial symptoms may be physical or psychological.

When patterns of busyness, gregariousness, and manipulation dominate our lives, we are virtually unable to question their consequences for our spirituality. All too often these behaviors are uncritically approved and rewarded. Persons who are rushed, even to distraction, are assumed to be doing important things; those who become anxious when left to themselves for a brief time are commended for their sociability; manipulators get good marks for being able to take charge. What such behaviors say to me, and to many of us as we grow older, is quite different. These are the marks of people who are missing their potential for a maturing Christian life. Rush, as the natural world clearly illustrates, is alien to a responsibly unfolding life. For commercial reasons plants may be forced to bloom prematurely, but they pay in quick demise for the retailers' profit. Inasmuch as we are, in God, also grounded in that natural world, we can no more avoid the price of violating natural rhythms than can a plant.

Compulsive avoidance of solitude reveals the terror of self-acquaintance. The fear may be rooted in suspicion of self-disgust or hesitancy about one's ability to make one's own acquaintance. Whatever the cause of the avoidance, however, estrangement can never be the basis for any spiritual maturation. The requisite honesty is simply lacking. It may well be that such willful ignorance is the precondition of the manipulation of others. Failing to value oneself makes it difficult to value another, and the circle of deception is complete. To expect aging alone to reverse these behaviors is naïve.

But while aging per se forces nobody to reconsider the continuing value of being endlessly busy, always sociable, and ever more the effective controller of situations, the fact of growing older often encourages such reconsideration. Life may begin to seem like a thread that is somewhat less well knotted than we have assumed. We have been led to believe that certain behaviors constitute an adequate knot, but we find that in fact they provide no assurance at all that our fragile existence will not simply become separated from the larger fabric of all life.

The prospect of death raises this consideration for some people and may be the motivation for overdue evaluation of the importance we have attached to widely encouraged behaviors. We may finally realize the need to cultivate the complementary sides of busyness and sociability. The knot that one feels the need for in the later years may be formed only when one insists on greater amounts of quiet time and solitude. Such may be the behaviors which assure that one will remain attached to the larger, ongoing fabric of God's people.

It is impossible for me to imagine that many persons will like uniformly all that they may learn about themselves in the retrospection of their later years. We are each an ambiguous bundle of virtues and vices, of achievements and failures. The point for Christians is not to be able to approve what we discover; we are not required to be self-justifying. What is obligatory is that we allow time for self-discovery and that we acknowledge what is true about ourselves. The justifying of lives is God's affair, and merciful we believe God to be.

With the abandonment of adulthood's pretense we are free, perhaps for the first time, to do some good with what we really are. Such is the high, beautiful, and modest calling of those elders who have discovered that nothing (no thing) can separate them from the love of God in Christ Jesus. It is a noble vocation, befitting men and women of wise heart. These are among the ambiguities which some people begin to recognize in the course of growing old. Enduring embarrassment and the need to deny what we find lead only to despair, which we may try to conceal with pretense. Alternatively, we may gradually be able to assent to the discoveries of our later years. Such ability is, I suggest, the fruit of faith in that justifying God who is no less Lord of our individual lives than of all of the generations. That God may make the case for our lives does not excuse us as we age from being increasingly clear about what we have made of them.

4

A Heart for Maintenance

I want now to make a more fundamental case for maintenance than is popular in our "throwaway" society. I shall argue that there is a precious wisdom in aging's increased attention to maintenance and that this is imperiled by the attitude that everything is disposable. Not only may this attitude and consequent practices be ecologically and economically unsound; they are spiritually perilous because they are predicated on bad theology. The notion that everything is replaceable—"don't repair; get a new one!"—is indifferent to the fact that life is not self-sustaining. Nothing important that I can think of simply holds constant. Things are endlessly changing: either being sustained, getting better as a result of effort, or worsening from neglect. To hold one's own or to keep any situation from deteriorating requires maintenance.

The need for maintaining physical objects is obvious to all: shoes need repairing, tools need sharpening and oiling, houses require repainting, lawns mowing, sidewalks shoveling. However complete the adaptation of artificial products, most things require some regular attention if they are to continue useful to us. In the needs of such mundane objects for maintenance we receive a fundamental, if modest, instruction about our relationship to the kind of world in which we actually live. This requirement of objects reminds us of our grounding by God in the physical world and of our need to shepherd things in order to survive. Adam and Eve's environment before the Fall was good but not self-sustaining: "The Lord God took the man and put him in the garden of Eden to till it and keep it [up]" (Gen. 2:15). Jewish and Christian spirituality is inseparable from the fact of our bodily existence in a physical world.

No less important is the need for maintaining human friendships. We attach great significance and effort to the sending of greetings and gifts on birthdays, anniversaries, and holidays. How to relate to each other in day-to-day life, how well we keep up a correspondence, how frequently we phone are all commonplace evidences of the need for maintaining close friendship. Blood relationships may be indestructible, but the quality and rewards of family are in direct proportion to the initiative taken on their behalf. The encouragement given to busy parents to spend "quality time" with their children is both a necessity of some modern life and a compromise with a past era in which families often had only each other to befriend. Simply being physically together is not enough to maintain a relationship. Ongoing and progressively deepening interaction is necessary to any relationship which is becoming more rather than less intimate. As there is no free lunch, so is there no utterly self-sustaining friendship. We have to be willing to give something of ourselves to any relationship if it is to thrive, just as we have to give our time and skills to the maintenance of the things of our lives.

This willingness to give ourselves to the work of maintenance is all-important. It reveals our basic values and the depth of our self-understanding. Indeed, it measures the adequacy of our understanding of ourselves as children of God set down in a world of things and people, a world in which there is no way to escape our responsibility for maintaining these things and friendships. If it is to serve us and others, the garden soil must be composted; the energy which it gave up last season to feed us must be replaced. If we are to be available to others for the exceptional occasions of great joy and deep grief, to say nothing of the more ordinary days of life, we need to make ongoing acknowledgment of our stake in each others' lives. Failure to maintain relationships assures increasing distance from each other and diminishing ability for true kinship. The importance of this maintenance for our world cannot be overstated. It is never enough just to *think* about our families or reachable friends or distant neighbors. We must acknowledge the importance of these varied relationships by specific ways of maintaining them, and for this we need hearts big enough to sustain the effort. Maintenance for which heart is lacking will not long endure. Not only must we love wisely, but we must learn to love and respect the maintenance that is necessary to support such relationship.

What is true of our relationship with things and people is also true of our relationship with God. Unless we are intentionally maintaining our interaction with God, unless there are appointed times and places for focusing our attention on communication with and from the Divine Source, then that relationship suffers from neglect. God may continue to seek us, as I believe, but if we have no program for maintaining our awareness—no time alone, no time with other worshipers—then we become progressively unaware of God's relentless pursuit. This is not to suggest that in our relationship with God, any more than in our families and friendships, our own efforts alone assure God's presence. With God ultimately all is grace; the work of maintenance is not the last word. It is, however, the immediate work—inescapable and blessed—of those who have heard God's word of grace. Having ears that hear, these persons have a heart for that work.

One additional hurdle to affirming the work of maintenance is the widespread belief that it is preferable to launch new ventures rather than to maintain what already exists. This is a quality of temperament more marked in some people than others, but most of us know the lure of novelty. There are men and women who might give generously to a new project but who will not support maintenance of an old one. Such willingness is not without merit, for there will always be the need for imaginative and caring innovation. But the fact that something useful is in place, and may long have been, is no reason for our being indifferent to it. It may well continue to serve human need as well as the new program, or even better. Clearly, a balance must be achieved between innovation and maintenance.

A

It would be unfortunate to assume that in one's later years the capacity for initiative becomes inoperative. It is at least as unfortunate to assume that those matters requiring and permitting initiative should remain unchanged. On the latter assumption—or shall we say presumption?—one often attempts to go on acting as though one had not grown older.

Whether in America what we worship is the cult of youthfulness or, as I suggest, the stability and productivity of adulthood, there is some combination of the qualities of youth and the abilities of adulthood which we revere. This attitude makes it difficult for us to approach aging positively. At its farthest extreme aging seems to annul the vitality that we value. Even short of death it involves preoccupations to which younger people can often be indifferent, and the most obvious of these is the time and energy which older people must give to maintenance.

As I write this, Minnesota is in the depths of a record-setting severe winter. I am especially sensitive to the inconvenience of such weather. Everything takes longer; many machines are balkier and clothing is certainly bulkier. Special chores and precautions are unavoidable, and numerous extras are requisite simply to survive temperatures that drop far below zero. The climate extracts a heavy price from those who ignore maintenance, as the headline of a recent newspaper article testified: "Be advised: Minnesota weather can endanger your life" (*The Minneapolis Star and Tribune*, 29 November 1983). As I have grown older amidst such seasonal extremes I have learned some things about maintenance: how necessary it is, how undervalued it is in our society, and how helpful a little initiative is in avoiding some of the perils of neglect. So important has this awareness become to me that I am willing to run the risk of overstatement: maintenance *is* our ordinary vocation!

A couple of misguided attitudes in our society may cause us to balk at this assertion. For reasons arising from national productivity, we are ever more prone to favor disposable items over those which require maintenance. In many ways this is undoubtedly good: durable tools of tempered steel are clearly an improvement over fragile bone or wood implements; inexpensive and plentiful books are certainly preferable to rare manuscripts available only to a select few in monastic libraries. Equally clear, however, are the public consequences of disposability, and litter is only the most obvious. What the availability of goods does to the psyche and spirit is something we hardly consider. Probably the most important aspects of our lives cannot be accommodated to the assumption that all things should be replaceable. For example, would anybody argue the superiority of dentures over one's own teeth? Or the desirability of a hard-won marriage over a series of ill-maintained liaisons? Of the variety of things which we rightly value, some are maintained only by our desire to work endlessly at them.

Equally serious is the misguidance we receive about the importance of creativity. Exhortations to creativity are ubiquitous. Almost anything that is different seems to merit praise. Amid this passion for the new and unusual, we may fail to consider the question of an innovation's enduring social value. Technological novelties, whether for the military or for entertainment, are of a different—and in my judgment, inferior—order of reality from those in the realm of the arts or from those political visionaries who desire a more just social order. It is tempting to assume that our fascination for technological innovation, which we readily label as "creative," is a drug to divert energy and imagination away from those areas where the limited human capacity for creativity might make an important difference to the quality of life.

It strikes me as fortunate that older people lack some of the qualities by which creativity is often wrongly thought to be nurtured. Too often it is assumed that one must await inspiration in order to be creative; the presence of the muse is the prerequisite. One hears this often from students who have failed to meet the deadline for a term paper. Increasingly I hear in such excuses a deficiency which is less characteristic of older people: the student is unwilling to acknowledge that for the present he or she is capable only of a certain amount of imagination with reference to the assigned topic. The youthful illusion is that one ought to be capable of something better than is actually possible. While this illusion is in part sustained by the desire for a better grade, it also reveals an unwillingness to be what one is. A virtue of growing older is freedom from such illusions. One is what one has become and does what needs to be done with what is available. What one *wishes* one had become is not a present resource. Paradoxically, in that combination of acceptance of what *is* plus the willingness to do what must be done— the letter to write, the garden to plant, the birdfeeder to build—lie the modest but important possibilities of creativity within the reach of most people. Nothing endures without maintenance; every creative inspiration emerges from the subtle interstices which are recognizable only in the loving process of maintaining something. The desire for some comprehensive inspiration reveals the absence of those capabilities and is, I suspect, the root of much tragedy. It certainly accounts for the immediate failure to meet academic deadlines. Whereas all people combine both limited ability and limitless potential for loving attentiveness, and this combination is the source of each person's distinctive creativity, tragedy inheres when the capacity for love's attentiveness is subsumed under the ever more inflated desire for unlimited competence. The combination of the capacity for attentiveness and one's actual present competence results in specific and good human acts which range from the ability to produce holiday pastries to doing the right thing in response to a highway accident. Excessive importance may not be attached either to the ability to pay attention or to appropriate skills. Both are crucial.

Our misguided emphases on creativity undermine the ongoing work of maintenance. So enamoured are we with novelty that maintenance is deemed an inferior activity. However, the later years of one's life usually require much more maintenance than often characterized earlier decades. In one's adulthood change is maximized: employment, residence, size of family, and other basic facts of life are often in flux. Maintenance is a low priority in this scheme. Unfortunately this particular image of movement tends to remain an image which people of all ages are exhorted to emulate. From this middle-class mind-set, older people are not immediately freed by the fact of retirement. The maintenance which was neglected in earlier years does not automatically become valued even when its importance increases as one ages. A climate of opinion is needed in which the elderly may gladly assent to the importance of the work of maintenance.

More attention must usually be given to maintenance as one ages. For this reason I earlier emphasized my conviction that if we understood our lives aright, if we had wiser hearts, we would know that maintenance is our ordinary vocation. We would know that the important things are not among the disposables, that creativity is a rare and costly achievement rather than something expected of everybody every day. We would know that without maintenance, most things—from machines to relationships—are deteriorating rather than self-perpetuating. We would be less needful of titillation than impressed by things maintained at their own distinctive level of beauty and usefulness.

It is often difficult to recognize the pathology in a societal attitude until one sees the injury it causes to some particular group. Our basically inimical attitude towards maintenance has that potential for the elderly. For them, as for those who would survive the Minnesota winters, the alternative to maintenance is death—either physically, emotionally, or both. Their very survival depends on the ability to take initiative on behalf of a little-valued activity. This crucial task of maintenance in the later years is fourfold: physical, intellectual, emotional, and relational. My strong belief is that if one attentively maintains one's physical and relational well-being, then intellectual and emotional health are sure to follow.

Some readers, feeling that intellectual activity is of great importance, may question this assumption. As I have suggested earlier, intelligence plays a continuing role to life's end. In its very nature, however, intellectual work tends to distance us from our personal life. That which can be done well only by some degree of detachment, as is true for the work of the mind and indeed for all productive tasks, is increasingly inimical to the mode of one's later years. Those who maintain relationships and physical health will be intellectually interested in many things outside themselves, but these interests will be empowered by self-acquaintance. It is, I believe firmly, also true that one's sense of emotional well-being depends upon the rewarding interests one has in things and people other than oneself. Again, however, such interests must increasingly arise from one's ever more accurate self-understanding. On this assumption some may discover the joys of a new activity in their later years; others may abandon that same activity as extrinsic. The keys to such discoveries lie in the attention older people pay to their health and relationships.

B

At the moment our society attaches great importance to physical fitness. Newly aware of the health consequences of sedentary or high-stress work, we all give and receive widespread encouragement to exercise. The U.S. senators who bike or jog to work are subjects of approving media coverage. All this cannot but be good for the elderly who, though their exercise may be less strenuous than that of persons half their age, need all such encouragement. Within an individual's limits, which only a doctor may identify, such activity is physically sound and emotionally renewing. As one who maintains a rigorous schedule of workouts, I suspect that through exercise one's mind also becomes more alert.

Some such grounding in the world of flesh and blood is the basis for the necessary work of health maintenance. Our God-given bodies are the temples of our God-given spirit. Such maturation of the latter as may be possible can occur only as we are attentive to our bodies' instruction. This is not to claim that they are our only teacher; Christianity is not reducable to physical culture. It is, however, to insist that our bodies are one of the important God-given means by which we are to learn about our true identity. In time, if we are lovingly attentive to that instruction, we will recognize that there are limits to what we may ask of the body, preparations we must make before attempting certain tasks, effects we may expect from things that we eat or drink. At the very least we receive instruction about frailty and mortality as the eventual fate of these temples of God's spirit. In the meantime, however, there is life to be lived by those who lovingly maintain and are therein instructed by their bodies. Life in the spirit is inseparable from our God-given bodily life. The fundamental assertion of both Judaism and Christianity is that the world, with all that dwells therein, is of God. There is nothing in all the creation that may not instruct us about whom we belong to. And some things, of which our bodies are the most intimate, may be more readily instructive than others.

C

The second initiative of maintenance is in relationships. As one grows older these often become both more important and, as physical mobility diminishes, more difficult to sustain. Returning by car late one winter's night recently from a wedding, I realized that there might come a time when such a trip would be impossible. That imagined limitation struck me as genuine deprivation; gone would be both the joy of physical presence at the celebration and the delight of the journey with good friends. Nothing, it seemed, could replace that privilege. This sense of deprivation was somewhat ameliorated by two further realizations: that the demands of such travel might come to outweigh the rewards of direct participation, however rich these; and that physical absence would not mean complete separation from the celebration still dear to me. Initiative would still be possible, and I could foretaste the pleasures of the next best thing to being there. Actually, by mail or phone I might be even better able to express sentiments than in person.

Our relationships, often taken for granted or neglected during adulthood, are critical to our sense of identity and thus to our well-being. While solitude and privacy are important ingredients of every life, the worst thing that can happen to anybody is to feel cut off from all caring relationships. Not to belong is not to be! Several years ago I officiated at the funeral of a man of my age who had lived almost half of his life in an iron lung. Paralyzed by polio in his thirties, just as his promising career was about to soar, he had reason to feel that everything he valued had come to an end very prematurely. The fact of his last twenty-five years, however, was otherwise. Physically confined to a hospital room, he maintained a lively interest in many of the world's activities, entertained and played games with his guests, and kept up an extensive correspondence with family and friends. Such persons demonstrate that rewarding relational initiatives can remain possible despite great age or nearly total debilitation.

All persons need to know that there is someone who cares for them and for whom they care. All persons need to be able to give of themselves to someone or something. Everybody knows the importance of the mailbox, the joy of the hoped-for phone call. It did not take Martin Buber to make us aware of the utter importance of friendship to our humanity, though many could profitably read or re-read his book *I and Thou*. There we are reminded that personal relationships with others and with God constitute our humanity. Such friendships are not an optional extra. Without these we are less than men and women. People of all ages treasure relationships, and as we age, we must not be blind to the possibly changing initiative of which we are capable.

Having spoken negatively about initiative in an earlier chapter, yet seeming to have reversed myself more recently, let me try now to indicate more clearly my understanding of its role at all of life's stages. The topic is inherently difficult because we are attempting to distinguish the respective importance of human effort and of God's grace in the work of salvation.

At the extremes we have those who contend that everything depends on people's deeds and those who, scorning such "humanism," insist that all is of God's grace. Both have had eloquent advocates throughout church history and neither lacks voices in the present. Arguments for each view are comparatively straightforward—and incomplete. Somewhere between these extremes lies a wisdom which takes seriously both the God-given potential for wholeness in all persons and, appreciative of the reality of the story of the Fall in one's own experience, the flawed character of every life. It is in their understanding of the depths and comprehensiveness of sin that we find the basis for the different evaluations of the efficacy of human initiative. Those who are more sanguine about the Fall attach great importance to human effort; those more "realistic" contend that unaided initiative is at the least ineffective, at the worst a consistent source of evil-doing.

Abandoning the consistencies of Calvin's predestination and Arminian voluntarism, the covenant theologians of New England held that while nobody is saved by trying, nobody is saved without effort. That is, the effort is not itself efficacious but it is evidence of the desire for wholeness which, they hoped, God would honor. How one can get closer to the truth of the matter is not clear; nor for now is that necessary for me. Until it becomes clear that it is utterly useless to continue the search human beings will seek for and take initiatives which promise greater wholeness. Many of these will prove quixotic, which may be a necessary step in the process of our salvation. So seems to have been the conclusion of a wise and widely experienced woman in her eighties by whose reflections on her life I have been deeply instructed:

> My long life has hardly given me time—I cannot say to understand—but to be able to imagine that God speaks to me, says simply—''I keep calling to you, and you do not come,'' and I answer quite naturally—''I couldn't, until I knew there was nowhere else to go.''
>
> (Florida Scott-Maxwell, *The Measure of My Days* [New York: Alfred A. Knopf, 1968] 107)

Yet even here there is an implied resignation with which I am uncomfortable. It suggests that ultimately there is no God-givenness in our initiative. I cannot deny that I feel otherwise: that though so many of the efforts we make become less than the blessing we may have intended, we must and will continue to try. Resignation destroys the ambivalence of human experience just as effectively as does hubris. The Christian task, as I understand it, is to persist in the search for initiative from the bottomless resources which God has granted to each of us. It is because we *are* God's children, *not* because it would be ungodly to do so, that we will and should be endless takers of initiative. The perils of this understanding may be real; they are, I believe, unavoidable.

Jesus' summary of the law exhorts us to love God, our neighbor, and ourselves. Neither in theory nor practice is it possible to separate self, neighbor, and God from each other. Who we are as men and women of faith—in our deepest self-understanding—involves our loving relationship to all three of life's ingredients. Inasmuch as they constitute our very being, we become something less than our whole selves when we try to isolate one of the parts from the others. All these relationships of caring require love, which I take to mean both respect for things, people, and God and appreciation for their intrinsic meaning to our actual life.

As children of God we have a vocation to steward our time, energy, and possessions so as to preserve and deepen all of those constitutive relationships which *are* our life. The exhortation to self-love, in particular, may apply to aging persons and their stewardly work of maintenance. Because it sometimes connotes unacceptable selfishness, of which the elderly are often accused, self-love is often neglected in Christian circles. Rather than being presented as one of the co-equals which Jesus urges us to love, the self is ignored, as if it is taken care of through the love of God and neighbor. I reject this common effort to subordinate love for self to love for others. Maintaining a proper balance among these relationships may be difficult, but to subsume one of them under the other is no sound solution, however commonplace that may be. Our loving relationship to ourselves is neither less important nor greater than the other love obligations.

The key to a Christian understanding of stewardship is in the God-givenness of our life in the world. So understood, we are unavoidably responsible for using our time, energy, and possessions appropriately to this God-givenness. Among these obligations, and in concert with love for all others, we are to love ourselves. I understand this responsibility to be the base for self-maintenance in aging. Self-indulgence misses the point; it is not just ourselves for whom we are responsible. But we *are* lovingly and respectfully responsible for all our God-given blessings. The care of one's time, body, relationships, and things is not a reluctant concession to sin. Such care may be but certainly need not be the vehicle for sinful selfishness. Selfishness is the antithesis rather than the expression of self-love; it is the attempt of an unloved self—or better, of one unaware of God's all-sufficient love—to overcome or conceal that uncompensatable lack.

Stewardly self-love is another matter entirely. A self-loving person has no bottomless emptiness to try to fill. That person gladly knows the God-givenness of life and is free—as a selfish person is not—to get about the business of living with whatever time, energy, and competence remain. How the steward invests these during a lifetime and disposes of them thereafter will express the depths at which love for God, neighbor, and self are actually lodged. Our capacity for stewardship will reflect directly the extent to which we are by love possessed. The responsibility for self-maintenance is important but never absolute. Its claims must always be in tension with those of the things of the world, our neighbor, and God. The assignment to be Christianly human is never easy. There is no way of simplifying the task of stewardship, for neither exclusive self-preoccupation nor utter self-neglect is an option for those who bear Christ's cross. Against self-preoccupation we are guarded by the realization that who we are is inseparable from the relationship with God and neighbor; against self-neglect by the glad acknowledgment of the value which God attaches to each one of us:

And not one [sparrow] will fall to the ground without your Father's will. . . . Fear not, therefore; you are of more value than many sparrows. (Matthew 10:29,31)

A Christian understanding of stewardship thus involves much more than money. However, one's possessions are inseparable from one's stewardship, and the later years provide a continuing opportunity to enhance the lives of others and to glorify God by the final stewardship of one's goods. How one instructs the world to dispose of one's possessions may reveal more clearly than any other single act the nature of one's heart for maintenance. In the instructions of a person's will are disclosed the extent of one's love for family, the institutions in which one was involved, the wider human family, and God. In such instructions others may see, perhaps for the first time with unmistakable clarity, how one actually understood the relative importance of life's multiple relationships. The prospect of death is the stimulus for personal honesty: for these I truly cared; for those I pretended a care which I would not now perpetuate. The potential for initiative endures to the final moment of truth.

With a single sentence in the Sermon on the Mount, Jesus put the case for stewardship as clearly as possible: "For where your treasure is, there will your heart be also" (Matt. 6:21). Finally it is all that simple. What and whom we love will determine our heart's devotion to the essential task of maintenance.

5

Longevity's Tutelage

One of the most productive assumptions in our society is that there are no limits to what we may become. Not to know that there are limits—or to be unaware of what they are—empowers people during adolescence and adulthood. The reality of our limits becomes apparent only as we try to exceed them. We learn by doing—and by failing. Contrary to much popular exhortation, we cannot become everything that we may be able to imagine. Most people learn this lesson gradually and without disaster, replacing the pain of lost illusions with the comfort of being more accurately what they are able to be. While it may seem unlikely to those still trapped in illusions of limitlessness, this gain is often not inconsiderable!

It seems self-evident that men and women will cope with aging more adequately as they have learned the lesson of limitations. Awareness that not everything is possible is basic to successful aging. It is the point of perfect balance between two damaging extremes: the refusal to be instructed by one's experience of limits and capitulation to the impossibility of improving one's situation through learning the lesson of limits too well. To those refusing the pedagogy of their experience I have nothing to say. Perhaps further experience will yet be instructive. Those at the other extreme, who surrendered too much too soon, need to be reminded that one's *attitude toward one's limitations* is at least as important as are the limitations themselves. Initiative is often recoverable when a changed attitude creates a different approach to actual limits. Illustrations are legion. In his 1984 State of the Union address President Reagan called attention to the vivid example of Charles Carson, a man not rendered passive and dependent despite a plane accident in which he was permanently paralyzed from the waist down. However tempted to give up he may have been, this paraplegic "works eighty hours a week without pay, helping pioneer the field of computer-controlled walking . . ." (*The Minneapolis Star and Tribune*, 26 January 1984).

Fortunately, few people are challenged by injury as dramatically as was Charles Carson. Most experience gradual diminishments, only some of which are immediately irreversible, though many involve progressive loss. Given this inherently unstable condition, which is different from other stages of life *only in degree*, there is the opportunity to discover what one has learned from lifelong experience. Such discovery, aspects of which were unknowable earlier in life, will enable some older people to achieve that balance of opposites which characterizes the wise heart. They will embody those qualities sought in the Serenity Prayer of Alcoholics Anonymous:

> God, give us grace to accept with serenity the things that cannot be changed, courage to change the things that should be changed, and the wisdom to distinguish the one from the other.
>
> (*Justice and Mercy: Reinhold Niebuhr*, ed. Ursula M. Niebuhr [New York: Harper & Row, 1967] v; the prayer was first written for the Congregational Church of Heath; it was first printed in 1943 in the monthly bulletin of the Federal Council of Churches)

Serenity, courage, and wisdom are among the marks of the psalmist's heart.

However exquisite these words of Reinhold Niebuhr's prayer, it is obvious that the ability to voice them does not assure their embodiment in a life. From numerous conversations with Niebuhr two decades after he first uttered that prayer, I know how real and difficult was his struggle to be serene about irreversible conditions of his own health. I recall vividly the occasion of his return to the lecture room after many months of absence following a nearly terminal illness. He was not then serene, because in that illness he had lost much of the exceptional power, both physical and intellectual, that had previously distinguished him. As he approached that classroom he was vulnerable as he never previously had been. In his study before that first lecture we prayed together his prayer with a depth of emotion which he perhaps could not have imagined when he first fashioned the words. A proud and wounded man, he desired on that day just enough grace to carry him through the hour. Halting in speech where he had once been torrential, physically unsteady where he had once been vigorous, emotionally uncertain where he had once been self-assured, he survived this lecture and hundreds thereafter. The price he paid for each effort, however, was awesome: nearly total exhaustion amidst some combination of rage at his limitations and pride in his achievement. The reward that he gave to others, especially those who had known him before his affliction, was no less precious. We knew both his greatness of mind and the struggle of spirit which tossed him between courage and reluctant acceptance of his condition. In the price exacted lay the source of our blessing. Many have since observed that the last years of this great teacher—in which his restless classroom pacing gave way to the podium chair, the finger stabbing to make a point became the gentler gesture of the whole hand, and the meteoric verbal speed became more hesitant—revealed the depth of spirit long concealed behind his animated erudition. In his advanced age Niebuhr embodied what he had long talked about: the grandeur and misery of humanity. By this gift many were enabled to affirm more gracefully their own strengths and limitations, finding serenity before the unchangeable, courage for what can be changed. Just such is aging's assignment, and in one's earlier experience there is, I believe, helpful instruction. It is not without preparation that God urges us to have wise hearts.

Our later years offer a number of lessons which, simply by virtue of long life, are within the grasp of any reflective old person. I emphasize their *universal* potential because all too often the achievements urged on the aged are based upon the capabilities of exceptional elderly persons. (There is a pervasive tendency so to inflate goals as to put them out of the reach of ordinary people. As in marketing, there will be no buyers for overpriced items. While I am not hawking bargain-basement goals for the aging, I want to state the tasks of life's later years in ways which suggest that they are—or almost so—within everyone's eventual grasp. Too great a gap between present capability and such goals will discourage too many people. How to phrase challenges so that nobody is "priced out" is a subtle and crucial matter.) Such exhortations, while interesting—especially to those who have not been forced to admit their limits—are, I believe, valueless if not actually injurious to most old people. Ben Franklin's inventiveness at age eighty or Titian's creativity at ninety or Granda Moses' works at one hundred are of little positive value. Many may laugh (or cry) at such reminders of enduring vitality. Rather than models beyond their reach, what the aging need are some evidences of what *every* old person may have learned in the course of a long life. And they need to be able to value these modest but potentially universal lessons. To achieve this ability may, in a society of other values, be the most difficult task.

Søren Kierkegaard suggests a clue to both the content of these lessons and their value:

> Life must be understood backwards. But then one forgets the other clause—that it must be lived forwards. The more one thinks through this clause, the more one concludes that life in temporality never becomes properly understandable, simply because never at any time does one get perfect repose to take a stance: backwards.
>
> (*Søren Kierkegaard's Journals and Papers*, ed. and trans. by Howard V. and Edna H. Hong [Bloomington: Indiana University Press, 1967] I, 450)

Clearly there is never a time short of death for the "perfect repose" which might assure complete retrospective understanding. Relatively, however, in aging life slows down somewhat. In combination with the desire to gather together some of the main threads of one's life-story, this retardation of time enhances aging's distinctive opportunity for review and self-acquaintance.

For many decades it is unavoidably the future which stimulates our efforts: the years of education in anticipation of a career, the basic commitments of family and parenthood, self-investment in work and public life, the development of avocational interests and skills. While the past is never irrelevant to one's success or enjoyment in these years, the present is largely empowered by what shall yet be. We live towards the future, which we often think of as limitless. At some point, however, this process slows down and we wonder about the meaning of it all. To discover that meaning, which can be an imperious desire, we need a different orientation. In old age we have the conditions to meet that need; sufficient time has passed and experience accumulated to enable one to review past years, to gather previously disparate strands, to discover the partly meaningful configurations and movements of life. We have the opportunity in aging to understand ourselves backwards and to be clearer about those matters which we continue to intend. Perhaps for the first time this work becomes an urgent possibility. We contrive until death to live forward, but in old age we become capable of a complementary posture. It is a wise heart which is able to incorporate remembrances and hopes in a living present. This is the route to becoming "fiercely alive," as a woman in her eighties characterized her deepest desire (Florida Scott-Maxwell, *The Measure of My Days* [New York: Alfred A. Knopf, 1968] 42). It is tragic indeed, as the Fool reminds Lear, to be old and stupid: "Thou shouldst not have been old till thou hadst been wise" (I, v, 46–47).

A

Among life's lessons are five which *all* people may acquire from lifelong experience: perspectives change; life-patterns become potentially clearer; there are "golden flecks among the ashes"; we do not control God's presence nor absence; and faith mandates endless inventiveness. While persons who do not consider themselves religious are capable of benefiting from much of this tutelage, it is central to my argument that such instruction is from God. Much of our experience may have been broken and episodic, but it is not thereby valueless. Our achievements may have been modest, our relationships limited and transient, our pleasures infrequent. Their quality in the past does not immediately concern us. What *is* important is that every person has lived so many years, so many thousands of days, and that all of these have been from God. This was certainly the psalmist's realization as he pondered the meaning of growing older: "Lord, thou hast been our dwelling place in all generations" (Ps. 90:1). Whatever the character of one's life, which universally has combined that which could and that which could not be changed, it *has* been lived and we have been given the ability to remember and reflect on this experience. Whatever else we may have thought was the milieu of our life—our families, our society, humankind, even our self-consciousness—proves ultimately unable to contain lives which reach endlessly backwards and forwards and which may, at any given moment, reach equally to heaven and to hell. A human life is an incredibly complex treasure, ultimately to be understood only as an aspect of the mind and heart of God.

Some may wonder about the validity of the importance which I attach to something as ordinary as our daily experience. This will be especially unfamiliar to those who believe that religion's intent is to wean us away from our mundane lives. Are not such lives, at best, little more than raw material which the believer is obligated to fashion into something more ethereally beautiful? Does not religious faith take our attention away from human imperfection and brokenness in order to focus on the beauty and adequacy of God? While there are elements of truth in both of these questions, I particularly oppose the assumption that God would not deign to be present in anything as ordinary and flawed as a late twentieth-century life. Such an attitude reveals only a fatal ignorance of that incarnation central to the New Testament and of Christ's assured presence in the Holy Spirit. If it is not to such lives as ours that God is sometimes present, then God is wholly and permanently absent.

My strong conviction is that we must reverse this all too common aversion to ordinary human experience. While we need not be confined to that ordinariness—indeed, it is Christ's promise to transform our lives—the possibility of transformation is directly dependent on our willing acquaintance with our actual experience. How can we hope to understand the presence of God to which others point from *their* experience? How can we expect to understand the Bible if we are unfamiliar with our own lives? Our experience is the necessary reality with which we must begin; and even in those lives most self-consciously averse to God or religion, the life-giving Spirit has been present. In the lessons to which the aged are called, and of which they may be uniquely capable, the work is initially one of self-acquaintance. As this work progresses, the reality of God's presence and absence will become clearer.

Both glory and misery are in all ordinary human experience. By this glorious ordinariness, this combination of chaos and order, accomplishment and failure, and pride and shame, each of us is instructed by God. No life so understood, whatever its achievements, is inherently superior to any other; despite apparent differences we all share most of our experience with all others. In aging we become able to realize that this commonality of experience does not diminish us. In fact, it is an often unanticipated relief to recognize how much experience we share with humankind. Without obscuring our distinctiveness, this commonality helps us to sense our universal kinship. We are strands in a rich tapestry of life under God. When we were younger we thought that we were apart from others or that we had to work at being special and different. Our need for distinctiveness was the empowering illusion. This is replaced in age by a more adequate belief: we belong. Gradually we claim both our membership in the human family and our status as God's children, heirs of the promise, by claiming the realities of our *actual* lives to date. Through acquaintance with our lifelong experience we know both our distinctiveness and our kinship with all people of all times and places.

This recognition enables us to identify the first of the God-given lessons from our life's experience: perspectives change as one grows older. The restructuring of consciousness is not, of course, confined to one's later years, for it happens constantly in daily experience. Think, for example, of your different perception of reality depending on whether you are the driver of a car or a pedestrian. Factors which influence perspective are legion and mundane, from environmental changes—is the barometer rising or falling?—to the skill of one's digestive system in processing last night's meal. Such myriad considerations, over most of which we have little control, cause our thoughts and responses to undergo constant modification.

For the most part these unavoidable, transient changes in perspective are superficial. Whether or not the sun is shining, and irrespective of minor indigestion, we expect people to be today essentially what they were yesterday. Ongoing life depends upon such reliability. In the course of aging, however, something akin to geologic upheaval occurs. By the gradual accumulation of decades of experience, one's consciousness changes. The increasing evidence that one's body is less resilient and more vulnerable and the deaths of others who are precious to one's identity gradually bring awareness of life's fragility and of one's own mortality. The effects of this awareness are not uniform; some will find more precious than ever the good things of their lives, and others will be progressively depressed. Regardless of such responses, one's consciousness is permanently changed. There is no route back to the perspective that was indifferent to fragility and mortality. Experience is a persuasive teacher.

Recently while my son was visiting us, he noticed on my desk a schedule of the dates of Easter through A.D. 2000. Perhaps because he had not previously seen such a calendar, he was pleased to note that in the year 2000 his fiftieth birthday will coincide with Easter. In great spirit he expressed the hope that we might be together for that double celebration. I shared his enthusiasm until it struck me that by then I would be approaching my eightieth birthday. Should I live that long I would exceed by far the ages at which both my parents and all my grandparents died. A betting person would not give good odds that I will survive to that April 23. Is it difficult to understand why the awareness of frailty brings both depression and a desire to make more of present good? My consciousness has been irreversibly restructured by a realization to which I came as a result of six decades of human experience. In the course of living my life forwards I have found the need to understand it backwards; and this understanding enables me to live more intentionally in the present and towards the future. God willing, there will be that double celebration early in the twenty-first century. In the meantime I have immediate opportunity for friendship with a son and others, and next year's birthday and Easter to anticipate. In my restructured consciousness I realize that who I really am encompasses generations yet to be born as fully as those countless generations by whom I have been shaped. Of all these, myself included, God is the dwelling place.

B

The second of these lessons is that as one ages, the patterns of one's life become clearer. We learn to distinguish between the lives we pretended, which others (and even we ourselves at times) may have taken as real and the lives we have *really* lived.

Two demurrers are immediately necessary. First, the distinction between our real and our pretended lives is probably not as absolute as I have implied. Just who we are is inextricably bound up with who we pretend to be and may well include parts of ourselves which began as pretense. As ancient Jews understood well, we tend to become what we consistently do. On this assumption they were urged to do the good even when lacking heart for it. In time, they believed, God would provide a heart commensurate with the deed. Contemporary behaviorists concur: change the behavior and, in time, the person changes. Second, because of the intermingling and mutual influencing of our real and pretended lives, it is at any particular moment impossibly difficult to distinguish accurately between them. Given the glorious and often frustrating complexity of a human life, no simple label ever accurately distinguishes the feigned from the real. We must admit the enduring difficulty of the task without abandoning it as hopeless. By the later years of life, however, enough experience has accumulated to enable those who have "eyes to see and ears to hear" to recognize some of the recurring patterns of their behavior and attitudes.

A death camp survivor persuasively reminds us that the ultimate sanctuary of the self—where we determine our *attitude* towards a situation—remains always within our control (Viktor Frankl, *Man's Search For Meaning: An Introduction to Logo Therapy*). Many who failed to survive the concentration camps died not because of malnutrition or physical punishment but because—deep within themselves—they stopped resisting their captors' inhumanity. Having lost their deepest connection with the source of life and hope, they gave up. In a few hours they were dead. When an older person begins to see himself or herself afresh, the attitudes of others become important. We can encourage each other in our desire for truthfulness, but the key to the desire to discern life's patterns lies within each of us. Although those closest to such aged may assist the process, they cannot bring it about. Inasmuch as significant others prefer truthfulness to pretense, they may encourage the older person's desire for more honest self-presentation. Such change in ways of relating in consequence of new knowledge of the other will be immediately costly to both parties, but such is always the price of greater truthfulness. Whether or not both enjoy the long-range gains will depend upon the importance attached to being present to the real other rather than to a person pretending a role.

Most of us are familiar with this poem by Robert Frost:

> Two roads diverged in a yellow wood,
> And sorry I could not travel both
> And be one traveler, long I stood
> And looked down one as far as I could
> To where it bent in the undergrowth;
>
> Then took the other, as just as fair,
> And having perhaps the better claim,
> Because it was grassy and wanted wear;
> Though as for that the passing there
> Had worn them really about the same,
>
> And both that morning equally lay
> In leaves no step had trodden black.
> Oh, I kept the first for another day!
> Yet knowing how way leads on to way,
> I doubted if I should ever come back.
>
> I shall be telling this with a sigh
> Somewhere ages and ages hence:
> Two roads diverged in a wood, and I—
> I took the one less traveled by,
> And that has made all the difference.

("The Road Not Taken," *The Poetry of Robert Frost* [New York: Henry Holt and Company, 1916])

What I take from this poem in my later years is quite different from my earlier readings. Then I failed to note the desire to be able to take both roads; the clarity of my vocational intent or the wish to appear so single-minded blinded me to ambivalences I can now affirm. Further, I believe that I completely misunderstood Frost's concluding reassurance. I took the poet to be self-complimenting, just as I expected myself to be some day. Now I see more clearly both his realization that there really was not much to choose from in the diverging roads and that, in choosing one, he was irrevocably declining the other.

In one sense Frost's final words are most important: the road we choose—and we need not compliment ourselves on having taken that "less traveled by"—does make all the difference. It is vital that one assent to the road taken and not hanker endlessly for the one to which there is no return. Where the poet may have been misled and where his poem certainly misled me as a youth is in his assertion that the road he chose "has made all the difference." For Frost, being who he was, little or no choice was involved. He took, as we all do, the only road he could have taken. The other road, which he half thought he was postponing until another day, was never really an option. Lives are patterned in ways which prompt us to take one road rather than the other. There is no warrant here for self-congratulations. Good fortune consists not in taking the other road—"just as fair,/And having perhaps the better claim"—but in being able to assent to that road which the pattern of one's life made inevitable. Such assessment, which does not require or permit obliterating from memory the road not taken, illustrates what Erikson means by the achievement of a sense of Integrity about one's life rather than being victim to Despair. A life characterized by such Integrity involves the ability to recognize the patterns long operative in one's life and, not without regrets, being able to see that *they* have made all the difference! The illusion of clear-cut choice may be one which age helps to modify.

C

Cousin to God's pedagogy through one's restructured consciousness and greater clarity about life patterns is aging's third lesson: there have been "golden flecks amidst the ashes." This expression is from a novel in which a prince, on his deathbed, takes stock of his life:

> He was making up a general balance sheet of his whole life, trying to sort out of the immense ash-heap of liabilities the golden flecks of happy moments. . . . Could those latter hours be really put down to the credit side of life? Were they not some sort of anticipatory gift of the beatitudes of death? It didn't matter, they had existed.

(Giuseppe di Lampedusa, *The Leopard*, trans. Archibald Colquhoun, [New York: Pantheon Books, 1960] 288–89)

The "golden flecks" may prove to be, as the prince discovers, many fewer and perhaps less shiny than one earlier expected. The important point, as Lampedusa affirms, however, is that "they had existed."

Even the most modest and vulnerable life is not without its "golden flecks." We need not debate the criteria for identifying these treasured moments; one person's golden fleck might be another's brass ring. What anyone recognizes as an enduring blessing will be largely determined by the circumstances of that person's life. Lampedusa's prince, who was not gifted at human relationships, found his golden flecks in his love for the dogs of his estates and in his impersonal astronomical research. Even so, the prince is uncertain whether time so spent was a credit or a debit. Inclining to the former—some "anticipatory gift of the beatitudes of death?"—he concludes only that thus he has indeed spent much time, and so he is partly shielded against despair by a shred of integrity.

It is not, I suspect, much different for any of us as our time winds down. Few great lives come into the world, and, witness Methuselah, longevity hardly assures greatness. Fortunately age allows one to see that unrelieved greatness is not the point. The golden flecks along the way enable one to ward off the demons of despair and self-disgust. Amidst the immense ash-heap there are many things we might wish had been otherwise, but each of us has done the best of which we were capable, given our inheritance and the circumstances of our lives. Even when self-destructive, we were doing the best we could in the light of what we could see and with reference to whatever resources we had to draw upon. Quantitatively we may all deserve condemnation, but the "golden flecks," perhaps infrequent and certainly transient, still shine.

Thus the aged can learn from their own experience that despite the evident imperfection of lives all people have some sense of useful, if limited, achievements. Few of these achievements are of historical consequence; most may not have been noticed by anybody other than the person who in a minor, critical moment found a resource of courage where previously only fear reigned. This brief moment made a "golden fleck" of enduring value which was not dwarfed by the universal heap of ashes. In life's earlier years one might have anticipated many such flecks, a crownful or more. That this is a youthful illusion, far beyond which one's maturation needs to go, is part of what experience would teach us. Most things are flawed, and no achievement is ever as innocently won as we may have imagined. But this realization of imperfection is itself no ground for despair once the folly of youthful illusion is acknowledged. Then it becomes possible to see again—as when I put on my glasses—the golden flecks: tiny, imperishable, and priceless. To be blind to such flecks will imperil one's aging, just as naïve expectations empowered and distorted the earlier decades.

D

In connection with these first three lessons we may begin to acknowledge the fourth: during our life God has apparently been present and absent for reasons over which we had little or no control. From our restructured consciousness and the recognition of our *real* patterns and especially in the acknowledgment of the ambiguous character of our life, we can admit that God has been at least as often absent as present to our awareness.

This, which we should have learned long ago from the psalmist, is very freeing to acknowledge. Intellectually from the psalms we realize that in the remote past people of faith struggled in vain to overcome the uncertainty of the divine caprice. Men and women of all times have wanted to have God under their control, which meant having God's presence and absence as *they* wished. However, God does not work that way, and it takes time for people to be able to recognize both that fact and the presumption that underlies the desire to control God. Whatever else God is, God is inherent in those moments when we realize how little we have ever been in control. God may be most importantly present precisely when we feel God's love completely absent— that is, when we recognize our lack of power to control. The intellectual realization of God's absence and presence requires that a person accumulate a great deal of ambiguous experience to be able to acknowledge both that God comes and goes for God's reasons and that we are incredibly presumptuous to assume we have an ability to control or even to influence those movements.

Only with the passage of many years of experience, which instructs one about the God-given resources with which men and women learn to survive varieties of adversity, does it become possible to recognize one's earlier misled and misleading arrogance. So often, in the seeming power of our younger years, we have spoken about God when we should have remained silent. In our hubris we concealed the divine reticence by all that we had to say. Ultimately—in God-given awareness—we become able to hear the emptiness of so many of our own words. Perhaps in this seemingly dark night of the soul we are for the first time instructible. If so, what we hear may be those words of the psalmist, "Lord, thou hast been our dwelling place in all generations." God has not dwelt in us; God has not been dependent on us. God is not our creature, appearing or not as we have need, speaking or not as we prompt. Rather, as Kierkegaard suggested in one of his compelling parables, God is the audience before whom we dance out the ritual of our worship and of our lives. We can only hope that God, as our audience, is attentive. There may be applause, but it will be occasional at best and always muted. In all likelihood such applause is the way God will be heard better by others, and what *we* hear from God will be in response to some golden flecks in another's life.

The lesson which aging has to teach us and which becomes less difficult as we have allowed ourselves gradually to be instructed about God and about life is that we are not the center of reality. All else does not dance around us; it is not in us that the generations have found their dwelling place. That place the generations have found in the Other who speaks and is silent according to God's own counsel. It is liberating to be freed from the presumption of what was always an inappropriate burden. Like Augustine of the *Confessions* we are free to consider again and again those many moments of our life in which there may have been golden flecks to which our arrogance blinded us. God's presence in our past and present is perhaps yet to be discovered.

E

The fifth and final lesson which we may learn from lifelong experience may seem to be at odds with the previous one. Acknowledging

God's reticence and the impossibility of forcing God's presence may imply that there is nothing to do but wait—as for Godot. Certainly waiting, rarely encouraged in this society, is an ingredient of human experience with which we need to be comfortable, and it is at least seasonally a central theme of the Christian life. Not by chance does the Christian year annually begin with the Advent weeks, in which we await again the Birth. Waiting is also something of which old people are generally more capable than are impatient youth. So the ability to wait *is* a fruit of God's lifelong pedagogy.

But the complement of patience is the capacity for initiative. This is the fifth of God's lessons: that faith in God mandates lifelong inventiveness. We must endlessly search for new, more appropriate, ways to view a situation—endlessly wonder about how things might be differently done—always in the interest of greater humanity and justice. These are not options for Christians of whatever age; they are imaginative capabilities which must not be ignored. We have from God a variety of gifts with which to fashion more humane life for ourselves and others even though, as our experience reminds us, there is no assurance that we will use these gifts as God intended. In fact the evidence is almost overwhelming that we will often misuse them. But this possibility is no grounds for us, however modest our opportunities, not to be persistently inventive in exercising these gifts. Although we often do not know the right thing to do, a fact which easily leads some people to passivity and avoidance, those who profess faith in the living God are mandated to imagine love's new possibilities in every situation. The dangers, as we see again and again, are legion. To be willing to run these risks, however, is faith's imperative. Neither God's reticence nor our reluctance to err excuses us from imagining anew and acting inventively. W. H. Auden has an appropriate couplet:

Ruffle the perfect manners of the frozen heart
And compel it to be awkward and alive.

In one sense all depends upon human ability to do these things. Against the dangers inherent in this acknowledgment there is but one, ancient protection: the recognition that all of our capabilities are from God, who is for all generations the dwelling place. In that image, which perhaps only the aged can enter, is the power to act and not to act as the limits of our imagination permit. In that image of an enduring dwelling place we can assent both to the limitations of our creaturehood and to our infinite potential: made in God's image, to imagine yet greater good in almost every situation.

The illusions of limitlessness with which we began this chapter reappear: in God we are capable of infinite inventiveness, even in advanced old age. Our need is for compelling images which are able to arouse our imaginations and to which we can repeatedly return. Such images can enable us to sustain the paradox voiced by a contemporary poet:

> But as I am I
> I am content to be what I am not content to stay.
>
> (Alex Stevens, "An 80-Years Self, Portrait," *The New Yorker*, 7 April 1980, 119)

Is this not the tension in lives at all stages? We would know somewhat contentedly the continuity of our present with our past and, for the sake of the future, not be content with that continuity. This is the work of love: gladly to embrace whatever has been, for it could not have been otherwise, while resisting the temptation to let that past utterly determine our future, however brief that prospect. Integral to our life from the outset, this tension endures to the end. It is evidence of God's indwelling presence, a reminder of the generations of lives in conflict into whose fabric our life is woven.

6

Life as Journey

Coming to terms with the journey of one's life is the central spiritual task of aging. Its preparation is the acceptance of one's rich legacy of self-understanding, the heritage waiting to be claimed by *all* persons. The legacy and the journey are available to everyone who ages, not just to those whose lives have been distinguished by grand or extraordinary achievements. However, in the simple, unremarkable acceptance of who we are, Whose we are, and where we have been, we paradoxically make of ourselves remarkable persons indeed. The willingness to care, be imaginative, and flow with the unintended process of life marks those older persons who have moved on into a new set of answers to life's questions. These are the men and women who have embraced life—consciously or not—as a journey.

A

One of the most important milestones in life's journey is the clear acknowledgment of one's spirituality. Certainly the meaning of our spirituality defies pat or glib explanation. John S. Dunne, a member of the faculty at the University of Notre Dame, has helped to clarify my understanding of the life of the spirit. In his book *Time and Myth* (Notre Dame and London: University of Notre Dame Press, 1973), Dunne distinguishes between life in the flesh and life in the spirit thus: the former represents the passing things and events of one's life, and the latter involves one's *relationship* to those things and events. This distinction moves beyond the need for awareness of one's past, to the issue of one's attitude or stance towards one's personal history. The crucial spiritual issue is whether or not one is able to consent to the truths of which one has perhaps reluctantly become aware: am I able, or not, to affirm what I now know about myself? The life of faith may begin at the moment when one remembers past events and does not know what to do with them. How one responds to such memories—either consenting to them as parts of oneself or denying them—marks either the onset of life in the spirit or continued life in the flesh. Thus the life of faith rests on one's ability to *embrace* the events of one's life in the flesh; it is not a way of avoiding or denying that life. Short of death, one cannot abandon one's life in the flesh. What is spiritually decisive is one's *relationship* to that prior life.

So much of what passes popularly for spirituality is antithetical to Dunne's position. Popular spirituality is usually highly selective in its approach to life in the flesh, preferring to emphasize those attitudes and behaviors readily approved while shutting its eyes to the complex actuality of all lives. This selectivity rightly causes many people to feel that religion has nothing to offer them: it provides no points at which to connect their actual lives to anything transcendent. Such is a spirituality of one's "best self" which seems to assume that all else either does not exist or should be ignored. The energy required to suppress so much of one's self leaves little other than that self-righteousness so repugnant to Jesus and the entire prophetic tradition. That such rigidity persists and even enjoys considerable vogue in a self-critical era like our own, to say nothing of its popularity throughout history, indicates the appeal of a life of avoidance and denial over Dunne's more demanding and healthy emerging life in the spirit. It may only be the truth which will set us free, but few gladly assent to the hard work of such liberation. Most seem to prefer the life of pretense. Such "spirituality" is often sustained by a mistaken assumption that bad things do not happen to "good" people. Thus the expected payoff for virtue is a trouble-free life. Would that it were so!

Unfortunately tragedies occur in all lives. Many of these are within our control, or partly so; others simply happen. A pregnant wife miscarries; a young person contracts an incurable disease or is the innocent passenger in a fatal highway collision; a health-conscious middle-aged person suffers an ailment which makes him or her unable to continue a career. The list of those things that just happen is endless, and it has no bearing on the matter of spirituality. The central issue of life is a simple question which all must face: can I or can I not assent to undeniable reality? The true test of my faith and my spirituality is the kind of interpretation I am able to bring to all the events of my life. This is the final task of one's later years: to take a stance toward all that has made up the journey of a particular life. Nothing of what has been can be changed except the all-important matter of one's attitude towards it. Disgust, despair, integrity—all these are possible responses, but the alternatives are not merely such extremes. Since all of us are somewhere along a spectrum between these extremes, we must realize that our goal is to be able to affirm our own strange mix, which every life is, rather than to be repulsed by our particularity. In every life there is reason for disgust; all have fallen short not only of the glory of God but, more modestly, of their own better inclinations. Life in the spirit addresses the vital but often ignored ambivalences of every life. As the incarnation and crucifixion should have alerted us, Christianity is a very mundane religion. It is about nothing less than learning to assent to our life in the flesh.

Nowhere is this worldliness clearer in Dunne's book than in the following sentence: "God becomes God in the moment when man becomes man" (ibid. 81). In fuller expression, God becomes the living God *for all men and women* only as we are able to consent to those parts in our story of which we have become conscious. Prior to our awareness of the hopelessly mixed character of our individual stories we really only feign belief in God. Or less judgmentally, prior to our need for personal forgiveness—in order to be able to consent to our own history as God's story—our so-called belief in God was really either an intellectual assertion unconnected to our experience or an expression of self-satisfaction uninformed by self-acquaintance. Much "faith" is grounded in a self-approval achieved by selective inattention to aspects of one's complex past. We remember only the readily approvable. By such selectivity, emphasizing only good works, we pretend a story which surely, we think, God could hardly fail to approve. How people familiar with the Gospels of the New Testament could imagine succeeding in that life which Jesus deemed fraudulent is impossible to explain (cf. Matt. 23:25ff.).

At some point in life, often later than earlier, many people become aware of their need for a more accurate knowledge of and positive relationship to their life's story. The roles which all learn to occupy, with varying and changing degrees of satisfaction, are often gradually sensed to be inadequate. Such roles, which are inescapably part of our life in the flesh, provide outlets for the expression of *only parts* of who we really are: for example, being spouse and parent does not exhaust one's capacity for affection and nurturing; nor, despite the efforts of the workaholic to do so, may we for any length of time use all of our creativity in our jobs. The fact is that there is more to us than others see, more than can be fitted into any residence or role. It is this "more" that, as they age, many people yearn to find ways to acknowledge.

To put this in terms of the life of faith, they want God to be God for them not just in terms of what is obviously good and true but also in terms of what is actually but less obviously true and less good about them. It is more of ourselves with which we want to be acquainted, and critical to such self-acquaintance is the ability to consent to what has been discovered about one's actual journey. With knowledge and acceptance one's past, present, and future become passages in a faith-journey, a life in the spirit. Alternatively they remain but life in the flesh, the journey into progressive despair. Such an understanding of one's life is not, at least initially, a matter of gaining control over one's fleshly existence but simply a knowing and consenting to what that life has been to date. To be unable to do so is to be caught in the unrewarding and ultimately exhausting trap of pretending an identity which is at best only partly true. Avoidance, pretense, and concealment are all inimical to life in the spirit.

The emphasis on self-acquaintance may be at first unfamiliar to us. People who think about the means of their salvation, of becoming whole, fall predominantly into one of two positions, neither of which includes the difficult work of self-acquaintance. On the one hand there are those who believe they are saved by grace, and to them self-knowledge is not helpful, because it is unnecessary: God does it all. On the other hand there are those, perhaps greater in number, who profess confidence in their good deeds. While these persons' "works" approach to salvation involves selective inattention to aspects of their story, their expectation nevertheless is that since the final judgment will be based on "heavenly scales," their good deeds will outweigh any lack of self-knowledge.

However, the means by which God may become God for us is clearly distinguishable from these alternatives. God is interested in the *whole* of our lives, just as we should be. There is no such reality as our "best self"; that is a fiction which does not interest God and should interest us only as *part* of our total story. But on the other hand simply doing the hard work of getting in touch with our highly ambiguous story will not make us whole. Salvation is not by knowledge. That gift is surely from God and is not the consequence of our efforts. Rather, it is a gift of grace, a gift which frees the believer to *undertake* the hard work. All of the liberating may be of God, as I believe, but what we do with what we have been freed to acknowledge is then clearly our responsibility. We are liberated by God's grace to be acquainted with our own very mixed story in order that we may be on firm ground to live in love.

Those who are inclined to depend on the adequacy of their good works need to be reminded of how difficult it often actually is to help another person. The ease with which we give help in an emergency may desert us when we try to be helpful in more complicated interpersonal situations. I am reminded of some advice given from a father to his grown son about the way to help someone who was in trouble:

> "By help I don't mean a courtesy like serving chokecherry jelly or giving money.
> "Help," he said, "is giving part of yourself to somebody who comes to accept it willingly and needs it badly.
> "So it is, " he said, using an old homiletic transition, "that we can seldom help anybody. Either we don't know what part to give or maybe we don't like to give any part of ourselves. Then, more often than not, the part that is needed is not wanted. And even more often, we do not have the part that is needed. It is like the auto-supply shop over town where they always say,'Sorry, we are just out of that part.'"

(Norman Maclean, *A River Runs Through It and Other Stories* [Chicago and London: University of Chicago Press, 1976] 81)

Reverend Maclean, as his son argued, may have made the giving of help too difficult. Loving his troubled brother and wanting very much to help him, the young man continued to believe he would be able to do so. That ultimately he was unable is a poignant reminder of the limits to our ability to do the good and needed thing. As Maclean also observed, "[I]t is those we live with and love and should know who elude us"(104).

We all know much more about our life in the flesh, which goes far beyond the obvious sins and limitations of the body to the misuses of the intellect and fanciful flights of imagination, than we are able to respond to. In varied degree we are all inclined to self-justification and are proficient at that rationalization which distances us from our actual experience. *Such selective self-distancing is the enemy of life in the spirit.* When we attempt to pass off part of ourselves as the whole of our being God cannot be God for us. We must first find a way of assenting to the complex, ambivalent totality of our lives, including our occasional inability to be helpful as we might wish to be. Inasmuch as we are created in the image of God, God can become God for us only as we are able to assent to the risky task of acting out of the wholeness for which God has destined us. Or to reflect the gradualism which I believe characterizes the Christian life, God becomes God for us to the extent that we desire that wholeness and, within present limits, to the extent that we are moving in that direction. The *direction* in which our lives are headed, not the speed of our progress, is what determines our spiritual health.

B

Christianity understood one central image as the precondition for human beings to assent to their full humanity: the image of God as forgiving. This image will prove irresistible to those who yearn sufficiently to consent to their life in the flesh. I realize I am hedging on an important question implicit here about the role of human initiative in the work of grace; just what determines "sufficient" yearning in any life remains imponderable. For now I am willing to leave the mystery unexplained. The Puritans, with whose tradition I identify, were content to protect God's power by insisting that nobody is made whole only by personal effort and achievement, but they also recognized that nobody was saved who did not try. Depth of desire is, I assume, the necessary if not the sufficient occasion of God's amazing grace.

The key to the double process of God's becoming and our becoming is a prior understanding of God's nature as forgiving. This assurance frees some people to move from fearful confinement in the ever-weakening life of the flesh to the more frightening but exciting and powerful life in the spirit. There is no way other than the cross by which we may affirm the broken wholeness of our life story. Thus while highway billboards may not be effective for all who view them, the texts with which they are often emblazoned are fundamental to any entry into life in the spirit: "While we were yet sinners Christ died for us" (Rom. 5:8). Until some such assurance seizes our imagination—until the image of forgiveness comes alive to us—we have but two dismal options. We can live either in belligerent defiance or in enervating passivity, both of which eventuate in despair. To move beyond belligerence or enervation—to begin to draw upon power beyond that controlled by one's will, to begin to assent to one's actual humanity—we must believe that God has fully identified with humankind, that God forgives. That we may become ourselves only with the prior knowledge of God's forgiveness is at least as true as that God may become God for us only as we become ourselves. It is impossible to identify certainly which initiative determines the outcome. Devotion ultimately ascribes all good outcomes to God. In the meantime, however, persons must seek resources within themselves which may move them in the direction of consenting to their life in the flesh. I suspect that it is always some combination of divine and human initiative which flowers as life in the spirit.

The journey is one way that we can move through life, but it is not the only possibility. Two extreme alternatives come to mind: casual drifting and following the tight itinerary of a short trip. My idea of a journey combines both the avoidance of a fixed plan and the determination to keep to the schedule of the tourist office; some combination of order and flexibility is probably unavoidable and is in my experience desirable. It is unlikely that many readers of this book are among the drifters. Those who have read to this point are more likely to have lived somewhat controlled lives, as I have myself. Their temptation is not towards rudderlessness but towards keeping too tight a grip on the helm. It will not be easy for such persons, as I am discovering on the threshold of retirement, to relinquish the well-established modes of self-presentation.

Thus we may discover the peril of having too clear an image of ourselves. However unavoidable some self-image may be, it always has two qualities inimical to life in the spirit: it tends to harden and it involves less than the whole person. Both of these make it increasingly difficult to integrate into the *living* present the full story of one's past. Too rigid a self-image carefully selects its memories and, worse, tends to assume that the journey is over. No further growth, no enlarged life in the spirit, is possible until we are able to relax this rigid image and embrace the full range of our experience in the flesh. The determination to be in control of our lives by controlling what others may know of us brings a premature "death" to the spirit because it denies the infinite riches with which the living God has fashioned all humanity. By declaring the journey to be ended, such rigidity blinds us to the fact that the journey in the spirit has hardly begun.

Both drifting and overprogramming preclude the discovery of life as journey. The former is too careless about the self, seemingly indifferent to its value made in God's image. All of the potential for good represented by that glorious image, all of the heights and depths of which such a life is potentially capable, are undervalued. Supposedly open to serendipity, the drifting life instead becomes increasingly insular. Thus is life in the spirit resisted. At the other extreme the programmed life takes itself too seriously, presuming powers of control inappropriate to a created being. If the drifter is content to make little of his or her God-given potential, the programmed person wants to ignore, if not to overcome, the limits to which all lives are subject. Discovering this to be impossible, such a person elects to concentrate on aspects of life and of the self which are so regulable. That such selectivity is judged highly desirable in our society is a largely overlooked cause of the paucity of so-called religious lives. The very achievements which we encourage, to which youth and adults are exhorted and for which they are rewarded, require that people must be something—often a good deal—less than their whole selves.

What God asks of spirited lives is comprehensive attention to the mixed ingredients of every person's journey. For in the spirit, the journey never ends. That is the great discovery inherent in God's becoming God for us. Our work is to reacquaint ourselves with the multitudinous ingredients of our life in the flesh and to assent to that recollection; we must integrate the remembered past into a living present. That this involves torment as well as delight is the inescapable price of spiritual power. Those able to pay this price will not do so only for themselves. They will be motivated to this painfully rewarding work also for the sake of the future. Realizing that neither their own journey nor that of humankind has ended, they will understand that their identity in the spirit reaches indefinitely into future lives, just as it has been shaped by countless generations in the past. The fabric of life under God must be so understood: both our memory and anticipation are for the sake of the living present. Accurate recollection of our life in the flesh is therefore crucial. It is because the journey continues that, for as long as we live, we affirm our stake in that journey and our responsibility to the future.

C

I now ask you to picture a woman in her late nineties living in a small, early Victorian house a few doors from the campus of a distinguished college. In a variety of modest capacities, most recently at the reserve desk in the library, the woman has worked for the college for about sixty years. She has long been in something less than good health and moves about slowly, with considerable difficulty. She has buried both her husband and their only child. She has little money.

On a typical Sunday morning in her house a 110 Union Street, we see a slowly changing group of at least fifty people, most of whom are students, spending hours lingering over a huge breakfast, enjoying animated conversation, playing and singing a variety of music. During the week too, day and night, the house is never locked; this is a drop-in place where a hearty welcome and easy hospitality are always assured. As a visitor here, one receives a cup of coffee and some chocolate chip cookies and is treated to kindly inquiries about one's family and—especially—about one's interest in cribbage. There is opportunity to look at the day's paper or to examine cherished scrapbooks of photos and correspondence from students of earlier times and now distant places. Watching and listening to this elderly, gentle but firm hostess, one realizes that she is both an ordinary person and a thoroughly remarkable human being.

This woman is Dacie Moses, a person who would not have been at all interested in what John Dunne and I have tried to say. In the first place she would have been suspicious of people of many words, especially words about religion. Futhermore, she would have thought it unnecessary, and possibly inappropriate, to talk at length about life; she simply lived it. Dacie knew in experience—and showed in her life—that the journey never ends and that it exists for the sake of the future.

The house at 110 Union Street was not always a drop-in haven for students. Not until her seventies—in 1957, in fact—did Dacie begin her tradition of hospitality which was to endure for over a quarter of a century. In that year, working at the library reserve desk, Dacie met a young man who was in the process of organizing a double quartet. He had the voices but needed a place to rehearse. Since the rehearsal was to be but once a week, Dacie suggested that the group practice at her house. Dacie's husband, Roy, was an important part of her motivation. Injured at work many years earlier, this gregarious man who loved men's choral music had become increasingly housebound. How better to perk up his spirits than by bringing into their home a small group of young men who shared his interest? Thus out of loving awareness of a spouse's need, an inextinguishable interest in youth, and generosity of spirit, Dacie Moses helped launch The Carleton Knights and a tradition of exceptional hospitality at 110 Union Street. One of my treasured records, with cover photo of them all in 1967, is lovingly entitled *Dace and Knights.* To perhaps everybody's surprise, both the vocal group, which still rehearses there, and the hospitality have outlived their founding hostess.

From these simple beginnings grew a tradition unique in my experience. Students who came because they needed reliable rehearsal space found themselves welcomed as in no other place in the intensely competitive college environment. Here was a home, always something special for those who live in dormitories, where the usual bases of acceptance did not apply. Who you were was always more important that what you could do—excepting possibly your interest in music and certainly your interest in cribbage. Is it surprising that the original eight young men gradually began bringing friends to the house? Is it surprising that the circle gradually grew, that friendships formed and romances budded? For many young people, like one student from Japan who has now gone on to a distinguished university career, Dacie's interest and welcome helped establish the confidence to complete a course of study that they might otherwise have abandoned. They were given the rare privilege of being befriended by a truly generative person: an unpretentious elderly woman who engendered in the young a sound sense of their capabilities, who nourished in them the vulnerable seeds of hope for the future. Dacie had her own clear values and set certain limits as to permissible house behavior, but these were always secondary to her initial welcome.

I will not forget the last time I saw Dacie, a few hours before her death in her ninety-eighth year. She lay tiny and frail in a hospital bed, and I stood gravely by her side for several minutes in sentimental thought about all that this wonderful person had done for so many. Partly lost in my own reveries, I was suddenly snapped into the present as a firm voice from the pillow said, "Hi, what's new?" Even near death Dacie was her same old self—sharp, interested, energizing. I could not hold back my tears. It was a moment, to borrow a phrase from C. S. Lewis, in which I was surprised by joy.

In Dunne's terms Dacie's life was a life in the spirit. Although she never articulated the fact, God was God for her because she had become herself—nothing less or more than that. Without indifference to the past and certainly with concern for the future, she lived as fully in the present as her health permitted. As she affirmed her life in the ever more frail flesh—though I never heard any more reference to her condition than a request not to hurry her afoot—she *was* life in the spirit. Consequently and with utter lack of self-consciousness, this elderly, unglamorous woman embodied Erikson's generativity: having life within her, she was free to encourage it in others. Because she was acquainted with the highs and lows of her own long journey, Dacie saw and encouraged others' potential for the affirmation of life's ambivalences. She had no inflated expectations either for herself or for anyone else. She simply nurtured the capacity for making something good, however modest, with her God-given capabilities and opportunities. Thanks to her sense of life as journey and to her willingness to be changed by its continuance, Dacie embodied the image which can allow others, as they grow older, to claim for themselves longevity's legacy.

Such was the long, last chapter in the journey of an extraordinarily ordinary woman. For seven decades she was hardly distinguishable from others of her generation. But a specific human need—Roy's for a certain kind of companionship—and imagination as to how that need might be met began a metamorphosis in Dacie's old age. Serendipity of course contributed—how many aged librarians get a request for a place where a musical group can rehearse? The qualities needed in that present moment, however, had long been developing in Dacie's unheralded life, and she was able to draw upon them for the sake of that moment and for a future whose extent she could not have foreseen. She continued to grow because she had to, but more importantly because in her life in the spirit she was free for growth to happen.

Dacie's final quarter-century was not all that mattered in her life, and certainly things happened in those latter decades which she could neither have planned nor completely controlled. What was important was that both of these were possible because of how she had lived in her earlier years. Something crucial, though possibly unrecognized, had been taking shape within Dacie Moses all the years prior to Roy's terminal illness. A good legacy had been accumulating. This character development kept her imaginatively open to ways to meet human need and, as her new role at 110 Union Street developed, enabled her to assent to it. Factors such as formidable indebtedness and marked lack of privacy might have prompted many an elderly woman to call a halt to her home's evolution into a community center. Something deep in Dacie's past, however, enabled her to assent to such a change. This ability to assent embodies the meaning of Dunne's life in the spirit. At some point Dacie acknowledged her relationship to life in the flesh, the passing things and events of every life. In that spirited relationship she affirmed to an exceptional degree the overriding importance of hospitable friendship.

Some such transition, possibly associated with the deaths of her child and husband, made the last decades of Dacie's life so rich and enriching. Lives, especially those of the aged, become either a blessing or a curse, not because of the abundance of things or the changes of fortune. We bless or condemn both ourselves and others on the basis of how we *relate* to possessions and experience. The roots of one's journey, especially of one's last years, lie far in the past: qualities of being, ways of relating to things and events are transmitted from generation to generation on the basis of those generations' understandings of their ultimate dwelling place. Dacie Moses was legatee of those who knew that "from everlasting to everlasting thou art God" (Ps. 90:2). So blessed, she blessed. The psalms' depictions of aging are many and varied. One poet's description of the righteous old is an image which we could profitably ponder long before our last years:

> They still bring forth fruit in old age,
>   they are ever full of sap and green. (Psalm 92:14)

Righteousness is not primarily a matter of right deeds. Rather, such deeds are the fruit, at every stage of one's life, of one's relationship to life in the flesh. If the things and events of one's life are known to be from God, in whom the generations dwell, one's entire journey—even or perhaps especially in aging—will be full of sap and green. Like a well-nourished tree, such a life will shade and nourish many.

D

One's last years, therefore, are of a piece with all that went before; not just in adolescence may one be "full of sap and green." The work of aging is to become acquainted with the nature of one's actual journey, to discover when and why the juices of life may have begun to disappear. There are, I am sure, limits to one's ability to reactivate one's greening. I am equally convinced, however, that these limits are not absolute; some recovery of the ability to yield good fruit in old age endures to the end. The recovery may indeed be limited but, the possibility of *some* greening is the assurance of God's continuing presence in even the most arid life. The harvests of our life journeys will differ with individuals. We are not equally gifted. What is asked of us in youth and old age is that we yield fruit commensurate with our distinctive gifts.

It is no more possible to separate old age from the prior years of one's life than it is to isolate any stage of human development from all of the others. At every stage we carry with us—either as burdensome baggage, useful resources, or, more likely, some combination of the two—memories and hopes with which to cope with the present. This combination of memory and anticipation is no less true for the aged than for any earlier time of life. The only difference for those who are old is the relatively limited amount of chronological time they may anticipate. Whatever time is available, the use that older persons make of it will be determined by the success or failure which characterized their progress through the earlier stages. We can continue to grow in the spirit, thus gradually enhancing our days, or we can allow those days to become progressively flattened, thus entrapping our life in the flesh. Such is the distinction between ennobled, ennobling journeys and tragic ones.

We do not encounter many people like Dacie Moses in a lifetime. I am fortunate to have met one such, and my life—like the lives of countless other students who knew Dacie—will never be the same. In the hope of helping others to become like Dacie, I have written about her here.

There are many images that may be useful to the work of aging. During those later years or decades, that work involves two related tasks: to become more fully acquainted with what has actually been one's life in the flesh and to clarify one's relationship to those multitudinous things and events. Given the ability to relate positively to this personal history, one may deepen or even commence one's life in the spirit. Alternatively and paradoxically, by the inability to affirm that history one will be ever more thoroughly in bondage to the things and events of life in the flesh. The damaging consequences of this imprisonment become especially clear when one recalls that the ultimate goal of all affirmative self-acquaintance is to be able to relinquish one's life gracefully in death. The journey through the world does eventually end.

For many reasons people may resist the self-acquaintance I am urging. Chief among these is the fear, usually well-grounded, that one's story either will not add up to much, certainly not all that one once anticipated, or that it will be intolerably shabby. The former realization—that one has not accomplished very much or has been successful at too high a cost—often prompts the earlier onset of mid-life trauma. Though some people are better than others at balancing the conflicting claims which inhere in all lives, nobody perfectly reconciles life's fundamental tensions. Conflicts between the needs of self and of others, the claims of work and of love, the need for solitude and for relationships, the imperative to justice and the need for compassion, the influence of the past and responsibility for the future, the reality of private ownership and public good, one's role as spouse and as friend of many are rarely absent. Ordinarily we function in our life in the flesh by acting as though one of these conflicting claims were paramount. There is no other way to survive; we can only hope that we have not repeatedly decided on the basis of the same preferences. Consistency in this regard is not only the hobgoblin of small minds. It is the means by which we demonstrate our indifference to aspects of reality which we are unable to incorporate into our self-understanding. To sustain our identity and modes of self-presentation dictates that we neglect parts of our God-given reality. Crucial for aging's task is the recognition that however partial the personal journey which emerges from our work of self-acquaintance, we are in this journey, as in so much else, like *all* others. We are faulted beings. This is the personal reality which we must learn to affirm in order to enter into life in the spirit.

E

Probably few readers of this book will confront such a task of affirmation as that of the central character in William Kennedy's recent novel, *Ironweed*. Having fled from difficult situations, Francis Phelan

had become a bum. Given to muscatel-induced hallucinations and repeated reflection on events which had triggered his various flights, he
eventually had a rare moment of insight into the repeated pattern of his
personal journey. As Francis was recalling two of the men whom he
had inadvertently killed, certain things suddenly became clear to him:

> The latter name suddenly acted as a magical key to history for Francis. He
> sensed for the first time in his life the workings of something other than
> conscious will within himself: insight into a pattern, an overview of all the
> violence in his history, of how many had died or been maimed by his hand,
> or had died, like that nameless pair of astonished shades, as an indirect re-
> sult of his violent ways. . . .
> Francis's hands, as he looked at them now, seemed to be messengers from
> some outlaw corner of his psyche, artificers of some involuntary doom ele-
> ment in his life. He seemed now to have always been the family killer: for
> no one else he knew of in the family had ever lived as violently as he. And
> yet he had never sought that kind of life.
> (William Kennedy, *Ironweed* [New York: Penguin Books, 1984] 144–45)

The ingredients of this fictional character's journey are much more
extreme than those of most people. Yet, however gross they may appear to those who, unlike Francis, have been able "to live peaceful,
non-violent, non-fugitive lives, lives that spawned at least a modicum
of happiness in old age," those things and events were the reality to
which Francis Phelan had to assent.

> Francis was now certain only that he could never arrive at any conclusions
> about himself that had their origin in reason. But neither did he believe
> himself incapable of thought. He believed he was a creature of unknown
> and unknowable qualities, a man in whom there would never be an equa-
> nimity of both impulsive and premeditated action. Yet after every admis-
> sion that he was a lost and distorted soul, Francis asserted his own private
> wisdom and purpose; he had fled the folks because he was too profane a
> being to live among them; he had humbled himself willfully through the
> years to counter a fearful pride in his own ability to manufacture the glory
> from which grace would flow. . . .
> In the deepest part of himself that could draw an unutterable conclusion, he
> told himself: My guilt is all that I have left. If I lose it, I have stood for
> nothing, done nothing, been nothing. (216)

Not many old people have so little to cling to, though all will have
some guilt to embrace. Those who truly live life as a journey, however,
are able to affirm whatever answers they discover in the end. The find-

ings need not be pretty; in fact, they will certainly be a mix of good and evil. Whatever their character, who we are in the spirit is inseparable from them.

As the work of retrospection approaches completion, few people will face as formidable a task as did Francis Phelan in the pursuit of life in the spirit. Many will be repulsed by their discovery of realities far less destructive than his and, despite the comparative beauty of their lives, will persist in their life in the flesh. This is a tragedy which I would hope to avert by insisting that, in refusing to deny what he uncovered about himself, Francis Phelan entered into life in the spirit. There is an incredible beauty and power in his willingness to affirm his ineradicable guilt. Though partly blinded by it to some of the modestly redeeming qualities of his life in the flesh, his eyes could nevertheless be gradually opened to this residual humanity by his painful determination to be himself in all of his guilt.

Francis Phelan was willing to be the man he was; thus God could become God for him. It is never otherwise for anybody. The depth and extent of the destructiveness discovered in retrospection will vary from person to person, as will the prospects for usefulness in one's life in the spirit. However, such fundamental truthfulness about one's humanity is the only firm basis for doing the good of which one is capable. The unacceptable alternative is to present, and to be present to, only one's "best self." In that pretense God will never be God for us, nor will we accomplish even that modest good latent within us. However much we may wish it were otherwise, it is finally only the truth which sets us free in the flesh for the life in the spirit that God intends for us all. We are, I believe, emboldened to uncover and embrace the truth of our actual journey in the faith that the God who journeyed with our forebears accompanies us also. This is the deepest root from which eventually flowers a wise heart.

Two episodes in the New Testament support this understanding of the relationship of life in the flesh and life in the spirit. When a devout inquirer addressed him as "Good Teacher," Jesus said, "Why do you call me good? No one is good but God alone" (Mark 10:17). At Lystra Paul and Barnabas responded comparably to the attempt of their admirers to deify them: "Men, why are you doing this? We also are men, of like nature with you. . . ." (Acts 14:15). It is crucial to be able to acknowledge one's life in the flesh for what it is: good but not equatable with God. That this acknowledgment in no way kept either Jesus or the apostles from works of love is clear from the report which follows in both instances. Jesus told the inquirer about the commandment and his obligation to the poor; Paul and Barnabas insisted that, though mere creatures, they were the bearers of good news. It is sufficient—is it not?—to be only what one is. The evidence is that God uses such truthful men and women.

7

The Other Dimension

Jesus insisted that the life of love, which is the human destiny under God, inescapably involves an outgoing relationship to God and neighbor and a positive relationship to oneself. This threefold obligation is more easily articulated than embodied, because the constant temptation is to subordinate one or more of these components to the other. Overemphasis on love of self is an obvious pitfall; such an imbalance can provide license for self-preoccupation and cause us to forget that we are neither self-made nor self-sustaining. Human lives, as Jesus realized and taught, are inherently interconnected.

Traditionally and with some continuing appropriateness, one's relationship with God has been given priority among the three basic duties of love. However, traditional piety is often very narrow in its vision, and devotion to God can sometimes minimize or obscure the coordinate obligations to love for neighbor and self. Illustrations of piety's potential for such neglect are legion. Because I am writing these words in the days immediately prior to Christmas, I am reminded of the carol about the devout tenth-century Wenzel of Bohemia and the poor man gathering firewood. Somewhat like Lear, this monarch, assuming that he had lived faithfully, learned that the truth was somewhat otherwise. The carol concludes with an explicit moral that reflects the king's eye-opening realization:

> Therefore, Christian men, be sure,
> Wealth or rank possessing,
> Ye who now will bless the poor,
> Shall yourselves find blessing.

("Good King Wenceslas")

True love for God is ultimately inseparable from love for one's neighbor.

We live in a society increasingly characterized by indirect services; for example, few of us grow our own food, and many of us have no idea how that is accomplished. The simple, daily fact is that we are maintained by our neighbor. It is no less true that whether or not we are able to find specific ways to render service we have a comparable obligation to maintain others' lives. This responsibility is inescapably mutual, and until this is more widely acknowledged by those of "wealth or rank" we will continue to have the food crises and social restlessness currently seen throughout the Third World. One wonders what, if any, vision will awaken America and Western Europe to the immorality inherent in the gross privileges which we so unthinkingly take for granted. It is, I suspect, excessive to hope that we will so far change as to "find blessing" in feeding the poor. It may even be too much to hope that self-interest will finally instruct us of the folly of our indifference. If history is, as I believe, in broad terms predictive, we will eventually go the way of all civilizations that refused to "bless the poor." Coordinate with our love for God, we are to love our neighbors as we love ourselves. This iron law of human interdependence is only temporarily violable.

There are of course some who act on their understanding of the deep interconnectedness of lives. Yesterday afternoon my family and I were in the process of decorating the Christmas tree. Grumbling over the uncooperative strings of lights, we were interrupted by a knock at the front door. Homer Robinson, an eighty-year-old neighbor, had come to give us a copy of a seasonal poem which he had written. He stayed for about an hour, reminiscing about events which we had shared and some which antedated our acquaintance, and bringing us an unanticipated gift of friendship. But his mission that afternoon included one more stop. He was going to the home of the local Red Cross chairperson to leave a check for the relief of the starving people in Ethiopia. An old man of no "wealth or rank," but living tolerably well in a small town in the American heartland, was moved to share something of his modest substance with people of whom he knew nothing beyond their plight. Fortunately this is not an isolated illustration of the sense of worldwide kinship that some people hold. Homer Robinson's contribution may not be the solution of famine, drought, or misuse and maldistribution of land, but it reflects a spirit that is at least not part of the problem. This man understands his connectedness to all life under God, as the last verse of his poem suggests:

Oh Father, thank Thee for Thy gift
Of which may I truly share.
I surely know I cannot drift
Beyond Thy loving care.

(Homer Robinson, "The Star" [unpublished])

A

The central emphasis in our earlier chapters has been on the importance in aging of getting acquainted with one's own story. By the hard work of retrospection one begins to be able to see the patterns in a multitude of situations which, over time, gave each of us our somewhat distinctive identities. I have insisted on the importance of this work both for its own sake and, paradoxically, because I am persuaded that such glad self-acquaintance is the only basis for constructive change in one's later years. Getting to know one's own story is the means for beginning to recognize one's connectedness to others, and the dynamics for bridging the distance from our own life to that of others are comparatively simple. Always one begins with progressive awareness of one's actual experience, for by recognizing the vast cast of characters within, one is also able to recognize kinship with the variety of others' lives. However unfamiliar or even unacceptable others' behavior may be, it is not utterly alien to me. I may not choose to act in the same way, but I recognize the sinews of such behavior within my own complex character. The fictional bum Francis Phelan of the previous chapter is not only my brother, he is part of me. All genuine learning presupposes potential for recognition. We learn only when we are able to see something of ourselves in what may initially appear unfamiliar. To meet someone—in a book or in person—may be to encounter some previously unacknowledged part of one's self.

Such recognition of kinship is thus experiential rather than abstract. We can be impelled to an effective concern for present and future generations only to the extent that we know, by recalling our actual experience, how we have been provided for at all times by nameable and nameless others. Imaginations so aroused will want for future generations a nurturing world comparable to the one into which they were born. So grounded in experience, and without illusions about our capabilities, we have access to often neglected resources, modest but crucial, for doing some good with whatever energy and substance we possess. This grounding frees the otherwise confined imagination and generosity to act consistently with the kinship gladly recognized. Once alerted to the importance of these ties, we will know that our possibilities for action—from personal benefactions to sustained political effort—are limited only by individual inventiveness. Homer Robinson and thousands like him do not necessarily hold the solution to the world's problems, but they are moved by their grasp of human interconnectedness to do *something* about the suffering of which they are aware.

However great or limited our resources for caring, for forgiving and being forgiven, their availability is directly proportional to the degree of kinship, the depth of commitment, which we feel. While feelings are subject to vagaries from which thought is often freer, at this affective level of our lives we "know" ourselves to be meaningfully connected to others. And it is from this "knowledge" that we are able to act, with such resources as we happen to possess, appropriately to the needs or opportunities of the moment. Thus, ultimately—and often immediately—what we do or fail to do reveals the depth and extent of our sense of kinship. This understanding of the dynamics of human experience underlies the emphasis on sins of omission in the General Confession used in many churches: "We have left undone those things which we ought to have done." Without heart we fail to do the good we might. It is about such capabilities that throughout life we have been developing wise hearts—or not. Either we have become ever wiser about the interconnectedness of our life with others or we have been progressively blinded to this inescapable and precious reality.

This other dimension of our lives is necessary from conception to death. Despite our deepest loneliness or intentional solitude there has never been a moment when we have lacked some meaningful connections to others. Their meaning need not be constructive or even pleasant, but there have been such relationships. One cannot be human without them. It should not surprise us that older people spend much time remembering the past. This is not just because they have longer pasts than do their juniors, nor even because the present offers so little of interest. Rather it is an appropriate activity in which aging persons recall with some mix of gratitude and resentment the myriad relationships by which they have largely become the persons they are.

One of the functions of church and synagogue is to include in their ongoing life men and women of all of life's stages. Central to the work of these communities is appreciation for the diversity of human lives and the determination to resist all efforts to marginalize any such sectors of society, especially the aging, who are most problematic for our youthful orientation. It is partly for this reason that the membership of many churches involves more older people than younger ones. Such elders are especially aware of the network of life's relationships, and given the comparative brevity of their remaining time, they are in the process of searching for those yet deeper memories which connect their being to the endless generations of humankind under God. With the psalmist they seek wise hearts; while not utterly distinctive to old people, such a search is often increasingly important in the later years. Faith's tasks are not uniform over the course of a life. Thus, because of religious communities' commitment to humanization from cradle to grave, for the progressive maturation of faith, they must provide environments in which the generations may support each other and offer mutually valuable instruction and support.

Usually we are more aware of those who have influenced us than of the influence we may have had on others. Often, for example, parents are surprised and disappointed to discover how little of something they deemed important and how much of something that was seemingly inconsequential their children have learned from them. They may have wanted to be teachers for good, only to discover that something else about them was what the children appropriated. I am among those who, in some instances, prefer my own judgments about highway safety to a strict observance of the law. Since our own children were licensed I have wondered occasionally about the instructive effect of my behavior as a driver compared with whatever verbal instructions I may have given them. This is not the only context in which I have recalled an old remark that is hardly confined to parent/child relationships: "What you are speaks so loudly I can't hear what you're saying!"

About a year ago I learned something about the unrecognized influence a teacher may have on a student. From the moderator of the church to which I belong, I heard that flowers for the coming Sunday were being sent in my name. Never before having been so honored, I was curious for the explanation. It was very straightforward but unimaginable. A man whom I had known as a youth was celebrating the twenty-fifth anniversary of his ordination to the ministry. Of those who had wittingly or unwittingly influenced him in that direction, I was the only one alive and still active in our common calling. In a wonderfully imaginative way, he thanked me just for being myself. On reflection it occurred to me that I had not been uniquely influential in this man's life; rather, by being reachable, I stood for many whom he thereby honored.

Would that every aging person might occasionally have such "flowers." For while life's other dimension is important at all times, being remembered is an acute need in aging. Many older people who are increasingly confined may cherish a drawerful of greeting cards as their most prized possessions. To visit such persons is to be introduced to their network of significant relationships. That a greeting card is often worn from much handling suggests how often it has been evoked as a talisman to recall some important connection. All people, perhaps especially the aging who lack youth's opportunity to meet many new people, want to know that they have been known and loved. At the least they *have been* somebody.

B

While it is undoubtedly better to have such positive connections with the past than to have only negative or diminishing memories, it is often the case that those relationships do little for present life and make one quite indifferent to the future. Inasmuch as a geniunely human life involves relationships *in time* as well as those in space, an exclusively nostalgic orientation to people and places constitutes genuine diminishment. It is the *quality* of our spatial relationships—the people, things, and sights of the world—which largely determines our ordinary ability to affirm the equal importance of past, present, and future life. The nurturing abilities of those whom we knew as infants and children and the life-enhancing qualities of the environment into which we were born gradually enable us to recognize gladly that the present is always being formed by equally meaningful past and future. Being able to trust the present and ourselves as agents in it opens us to the resources of memory and hope. The dimensions of space and time provide the contexts within which we become certain kinds of human beings. Commenting on a recent film by distinguished Scots movie maker, Bill Forsyth, a critic observed that *Comfort and Joy* "illustrates that significant decisions of who we are and what is important to us result from choices arising out of bromidic and serendipitous events" (Frederick Brussat, *Cultural Information Service*, 12 October 1984). Hardly recognizing them as choices and blind to their cumulative effect, we become through small things one kind of person rather than another. We tend to be more aware of an imbalance within either context—such as the temptation to value things over people or the preference for remembering over anticipating—than of the need to maintain a balance between the claims of time and space. But neither may be ignored with impunity.

Nor can the two be wholly separated, for each has a bearing on the other. Take, for example, the spatial consideration of housing for the aged. Certainly, older people enjoy each other's company and should have access to it; the generational memories which they share make friendships come more easily. However, there is no Christian rationale for isolating old people in ghettos, no matter how grand such housing may be. For their human well-being they need, as do people of all ages, contact with men and women of generations other than their own. I was struck in conversation with public officials in Norway by their insistence that old people should be housed in apartment buildings occupied by families including persons of all ages. This *inclusive* occupancy illustrates an expression used years ago by a friend: "Good design is God's design." In order to be *for* each other—that is, mutually instructive and influencing—the generations need to be *with* each other. It is that simple. We move in that direction as we encourage programs like Adopt-a-Grandparent or Adopt-a-Grandchild. By such opportunities for direct and continuing contact with younger adults and children, as well as by association with others of their own generation, older people are encouraged to keep past, present, and future in lively interaction. This understanding of time's dimensions protects aging from the flattening effect of preoccupation with only the past. What sense we are able to make of time's components is absolutely critical to our humanity, and at different stages of our lives we lose the balance by assuming that either future or present or past is sufficient unto itself. The nature of the potential for such imbalance varies from cradle to grave; its effects, however, uniformly diminish our grasp of the human task and potential.

Aging's ordinary temptation is to lose the balance by progressive preoccupation with the past. That individual lives are thereby diminished must be clear and is taken for granted here. What is less obvious is the effect of this diminishment on older people's involvement in what we are calling the other dimension. By attempting to live largely in the past, remembering people who may be long dead and places that have significantly changed, such as the isolated swimming hole of one's youth now surrounded by split-level houses, one becomes less attentive to present opportunities for meaningful friendships and also to one's responsibility for assuring the availability of a nurturing environment for future generations. By neglect one gradually loses one's social skills; isolation from younger people, especially children, can also make one lose whatever motivation one may have had for providing a better world, or at least as good a world as one received, for today's young. Increasing preoccupation with one's yesterdays darkens the glass of both this day and the next.

Regrettably, this pattern of diminishment—of living only with yesterday's others—is all too characteristic of many old people. Wrongly assuming that they would not live to an old age, they may have been indifferent to the cumulative effect of their particular way of keeping an imbalance of time's components. In this indifference they betrayed their vocation from God and incorrectly assumed that they could do so with impunity. There are a variety of ways in which to practice such imbalance. Some people may have thought that they could live without reference to the past; they may have ignored the organic causes of family deaths and thereby failed to take precautions appropriate to their genetic inheritance, or they may have neglected to keep any record of experience on the assumption that, if needed, they could recall it at will—only to discover its eventual, sometimes unrecoverable, importance to them. No less common, at least among youth, is the tendency to live only for the future. Instruction from present experience and even its enjoyment are viewed largely as instrumental to future well-being. The trouble is that through long ignorance we lose the capacity for connecting with the present as the only lively moment to which we ever have access. We are naïve about the vital need to keep in touch with the triad of time's dimensions. In a journal during her seventy-first year, during a summer in which she had an endless succession of houseguests, May Sarton recorded this observation: ". . . I realize acutely that solitude is my element, and the reason is that extreme awareness of other people . . . precludes awareness of one's self, so after a while the self no longer knows that it exists" (May Sarton, *At Seventy: A Journal* [New York and London: W. W. Norton and Co., 1984] 171). Her understandable reaction to the obligations of so much entertaining is possibly overstated, but it is a vivid reminder of the need to give adequate time and attention to both others and self.

Our physical bodies tend to thrive with exercise and become progressively limited by its neglect. Like the renewability of those bodies, the potential for recovering time's components is probably never wholly lost but must be paid for by more strenuous effort when long neglected than we ordinarily recognize. What, for example, might a person have to do to recover a meaningful sense of the future after years of life oriented only to present or past? By "meaningful" I refer not to just the intellectual realization that time stretches ahead. Such awareness per se does nothing to enhance an outlook which prefers to dwell in memory alone. For the future to be meaningful it must hold some potential for enhancing one's life and life generally. For example, some people are animated for present life by the image of their eventual membership in the "communion of saints." Others, like the Gray Panthers, are energized by their identification with present and future generations of the aging and by yet broader concern for a more just and humane society.

The cumulative effect of decades of inattention to time's balancing act or of indifference to one's particular imbalance which may have persisted over generations in given families or even longer in societies, is often a subtle change of character. Seldom do we think about what is happening to us as persons, who may one day be old, as the result of our particular way of thinking about and acting with conscious reference to the past, present, and the future. Too rarely do we reflect on the implications of our attitudes towards memory and hope for the liveliness or morbidity of our present days. Unfortunately it is possible to be long indifferent to our particular imbalance of time's components. Not until their last years do many people recognize with regret the consequences of the imbalance they have long ignored. Undeniably we are human beings whose connectedness to past and future is intrinsic to our well-being.

Some few people first bump into these realities in the context of their jobs, though not all work holds the potential for being so instructive. In an industrialized society the demands and the rewards of most employment reveal quickly what they ask of us and have to offer. Within a few weeks at the most one can expect to know all that is important about one's job. Selling might be a case in point. If able-bodied and willing, one will likely be qualified for the work indefinitely. Whether or not one senses that she or he will be long satisfied *doing* such work will be determined by such intrinsic factors as personal ambition and those more job-extrinsic, such as colleagues and the opportunity for extracurricular activities. In Britain, for example, I observed that widespread labor unrest was somewhat ameliorated by employment-based sports facilities and teams.

Within the ancient professions and perhaps in modern forms of work sometimes designated "professional," the dynamics are quite different. It is common knowledge that the time required to qualify for such employment may seem endless: fifteen years after high school is not exceptional for the board-certified doctor. Even public school teaching requires not only the bachelor's degree but continuing education over the course of a career. What is less commonly known, often even by those who suffer its adversity—and especially those loath to admit that they may have made a bad choice—is that professional or artistic work may take as much time *after* qualification as before to reveal its real demands and rewards. In a society overimpressed by income and the privileges which wealth permits, it is taken for granted that work which pays extremely well must be satisfying. For some professionals the financial reward is quite sufficient. Inasmuch as wealth was their primary motivation for undertaking the arduous necessary training they will, at least temporarily, begin gladly to reap the rewards of their diligence. It may not be until much later, when the pleasures associated with wealth have begun to wane, that they find themselves uncertain about their desire to remain in their careers. This is a circumstance calling for patience and deep understanding on the part of those who are the significant others in the life of professional persons so unsettled. Probably it is the circumstance which best explains such problems as the high incidence of alcoholism and drug abuse in the medical profession and the abandonment of ministry by those in the church. The doctor or minister has discovered some of the time-released secrets of the practice of a profession and wonders if he or she has the heart for it. The issues are intrinsic to the work itself, thereby raising the most disturbing questions for the practitioner. However possible it may earlier have been to find compensating satisfactions in the extrinsic privileges which accrue to professional people, these benefits are progressively unable to shield one from the probing uncertainty about one's ability to find sufficient motivation for the tasks.

Some forms of work, the extensive preparation for which often fails to pose adequately the questions of a candidate's fitness for that professional life, only gradually disclose the demands which are inseparable from them. Wherever fitness is understood narrowly as academic competence, the sorts of questions once posed for clergy in terms of the depths of one's calling fail to be asked. Thus, in the highly paid professions, it is assumed that the combination of personal ambition and accredited competence will be sufficient to sustain one in a long career. For some, perhaps many, such motivation proves sufficient. Others initially so motivated discover that there are demands inseparable from the work for which they progressively lack heart.

The analogy which I am suggesting in this lengthy illustration may now be stated simply: as some professionals find that they lack the resources for continued intentionality, so some older persons discover that the time-imbalance of their past renders them unable to embrace with equal enthusiasm the components of past, present, and future. Like the professionals who discover lack of motivation for the work, such aging persons have invested decades in living according to a certain imbalance. Neither is likely immediately to abandon the partial satisfaction and competencies they have acquired in so living: one in professional training and experience, the other in a variety of life circumstances. Both suffer the consequences of failure to ask about more than the adequacy of their training and experience for the long haul. For example, do I have the heart for the intrinsic demands of such work over the course of a lifetime? As is true in the professions, for most people life only gradually reveals its deep demands and true rewards. Surely it is nothing less than tragic for any person to reach a point where the real, unanticipated demands reveal that prior preparation has left one with deficient intention for the tasks. This is no casual self-confrontation. It is the stuff which yields either despair or, more rarely, the willingness to pay the high cost of attempting to modify, in degree at least, the imbalance which rendered one unable to undertake the peculiar agenda of one's later years. At the deepest level for every person we are faced with the question of our vocation under God.

C

Most talk about vocation refers to the work that people do in the world. It is true of course that Christian vocation does include a person's work, but this is not its deepest meaning. Primarily vocation refers to one's relationship with God.

We cannot escape the fact of God, both in terms of claims upon us and of the resources with which we are provided. There are demands built into life from which most of us will shy away unless we can draw upon powers greater than those to which we ordinarily have access. In saying this I do not refer to resources *outside* ourselves. Rather, each of us has God-given capabilities that we are able to draw upon only inasmuch as we know ourselves to be meaningfully related to God. Many of us, for example, will be satisfied with too little independence because we quickly see the dangers of taking freedom seriously. Most of us will persuade ourselves that a little bit of self-understanding is sufficient, and we will try to be content with an occasional kindness toward our neighbor. We will do this rather than try to live with the realization that freedom *is* God's intent for us, that self-understanding is among the privileges of our humanity, and that the neighbor is the person given to us by God for the achievement of that humanity. Inasmuch as my observations about our timidity and prudence are accurate, they indicate that we are not free to become fully the men and women we might be. We may see what is needed in a given situation—it may be greater assertion of freedom or a sleepless night in search of greater self-understanding—but we compromise because the price asked of us is more than we are willing to pay. If we are going to become in our later years the persons we were made to be, we need deeper grounding for our lives than mere self-interest and we need deeper courage and determination than most of us ordinarily possess. Usually, to awaken people to potential resources greater than their own is to urge them to "turn to God." This expression, though valid, is misleading. It suggests a source of empowerment *outside* ourselves—like a gasoline generator for power emergencies—which we may plug into. I prefer to think of our relationship to God as the means by which we are freed to draw upon otherwise inaccessible, God-given resources *within* *ourselves*.

The great claim of Christian faith is that God desires for us the fullest life of which we are capable and that, in Jesus Christ, God provides both the model and the power by which such maturity may be abundantly achieved (cf. John 10:10). That people have responded to such a liberated humanity is the testimony of all ages and places; that the first stage in one's progress toward such a humanity is a growing self-understanding is equally clear to me. Many, however, are as much repulsed by Christian adulthood as they are attracted by it, because they realize that it will call for significant changes in their lives. It is no less sad nor less true that we are frightened by self-understanding for many of the same reasons. While self-understanding is only the first stage toward the Christian life—initially it can only make us aware of the forces which confine us—we often begin to back away soon after the process has begun.

Within us are conflicting impulses toward self-understanding. As we emerge from childhood and are granted increasing measure of freedom, we realize the need for greater self-awareness than was true for us as children. The need to make decisions and the privilege of establishing relationships impels us to deeper self-consciousness. This is normally inevitable, and despite the fact that the process is often painful and frustrating, it is good. It is the only way by which we move from a life largely directed by other people to one in which we assume greater responsibility for ourselves. The conflict arises, however, when we begin to see some of the dangers and the endlessness of the process. To rejoice in freedom from parental restraint is one thing; to be able to accept the demands for self-understanding which accompany that freedom is quite another matter. Self-understanding demands both discipline and imagination if the widest context for our life is to be encompassed. It calls for discipline because we must make persistent and painstaking efforts to become aware of the various ingredients which shape our interests and attitudes. To become responsibly self-aware means that one must learn both to know and to view critically these very interests and attitudes which are so much a part of us. Self-understanding also requires imagination, as we are called upon to be able to view life from the perspective of others, of whom God is central, and as we must forever extend the range of life to which we acknowledge ourselves meaningfully related.

The great temptation in becoming aware of the serious inadequacies of a merely self-centered world is to refuse to pay the price of moving beyond such narrowness. This awareness of deficiency and the refusal to do anything about it is sin. It is the rejection of God's call to become more humane. It is the attempt to identify present, partial life with the wholeness of which we are capable. Rejecting this vocation is harmful because we thus obscure the very conditions by which our humanity can be enlarged. We withdraw from the possibility of life because of our reluctance to pay the cost. This rejection is also harmful to others, for it causes the vast capacities which we possess to be improperly directed towards those around us. When our powers to build up life both in ourselves and in others are misdirected, they not only fail to serve the right purposes: they disserve them.

Thus on the one hand we have the great claim of Christian faith that there is a humanity, a true vocation, to which we are called by God in Jesus Christ. This vocation liberates us for a creative and responsible approach to our lives. Self-understanding does not of itself give us that new life in Christ; we are not saved by what we know even about ourselves. Rather, that wholeness involves our *positive relationship* to what we do know, and that relationship is God's gift to us if we will have it. Given a growing self-awareness and the knowledge that there is a liberated humanity to which God would call us, we have the conditions which may enable us to move beyond the boredom of a life centered upon ourselves. These facts demonstrate the peril of the temptation to reject the self-understanding which God encourages. Only when we as adults are painfully aware of the deficiency of our life does God have opportunity to lure us more deeply into that freedom which is our true vocation. Not until we are dissatisfied with all else, not until we are aware of the insufficiency of humanity on any other basis, does the possibility of God's liberation become alive for us. It is impossible to risk the life of faith until we recognize that God is faithful and that only in that relationship will we know we belong unalterably to the God-given world of people and nature. We will try every other possibility, ways which both demand and offer less, before responding to that calling of God which requires so much and rewards us so much more generously.

Much of this is incomprehensible to youth. And the problem is rooted in the very fact of their age, for such faith as the young possess is essentially imitative. It has not been forged out of personal experience; it is not the result of a long search for the deepest foundation upon which to construct a life. The faith of youth, perhaps especially American youth of our own time who have been shielded from so much that helped bring maturity sooner to earlier generations, is largely an imitation of the religious practice and attitudes of their elders. It is their parents, often themselves examples of superficial church membership, who provide the models of Christian life. Yet few parents are able to convey to their children both the resources which they find in Christian faith and the doubts by which they are both plagued and stimulated to growth. Must we not recognize that that faith is largely the product of crises through which one has lived? Faith does not come into existence all on its own, independent of issues and experiences of the past, nor does it continue without reference to critical questions of the present. But especially for those who feel obliged to assure the young of their certainties, it is never easy to share unsettling experiences with one's children. Consequently children tend to see and to imitate only the religious externals of their parents, forms which do not sustain the young because these externals do not clearly evince a relationship to God derived from crucial personal experience. That which most deeply underlies a vital adult faith is often concealed from others under the forms of religious observance.

It is largely for this reason that a good deal of religious "wrenching" goes on during adolescence. It need not be the case that the parental religious faith was inauthentic, though this is often partly true. Rather, the trials of one generation, out of which came a more or less mature faith, are not the identical trials of their successors. The wars and Depression early in this century are of little immediate significance to those coming of age today. Thus the faith which sustains the former generation cannot be transferred in an undisturbed way to their children. The problems at this point are obviously complicated by the fact that the young often feel excessively restrained by their elders and are tempted, in their desire for liberation, to cast off the religious tradition as nothing but an ingredient of the repressive authority from which they must be free. It takes about three generations for a vital, experience-derived faith to become empty. The son mimes the behavior of his faith-energized father; finding no energy in his father's imitative behavior, the grandson does not bother with church observance at all.

Thus in reviewing and often discarding the imitative religious patterns of the younger years, a teenager may obscure the fact that rejection of parental patterns and authority is not necessarily rebellion against God. Some parents might not like the idea, but does not God support and encourage this liberation? While it would be inaccurate to say that God opposes any and all restraints which are imposed upon people, it is true that faith in God cannot be based upon mere imitation of the practice of one's parents. All of us must learn for ourselves what the issues of belief and nonbelief involve, and we can do this only by taking responsibility for our own lives. Almost unavoidably this means liberation from parents, however wise and well-meaning they may be, in order that the emerging persons may discover for themselves the excitement and the peril of making decisions. The regrettable fact is that youth often make at least two false assumptions as they go about the process of becoming free adults: they wrongly assume both that God is either not interested in this process or is opposed to it and that they possess within themselves the resources to carry through the process of self-understanding which began with their struggle for liberation. God is assumed to oppose the freedom which adulthood demands because, after all, the commandment says to honor one's father and mother. While this is not the place to enter into full discussion of the importance and meaning of this commandment, I would think it self-evident that to honor parents could not mean the same thing at age ten as at twenty or at seventy. As one whose parents have long been dead, I obviously cannot honor my mother and father as I might once have done. I can and do cherish their memories. Beyond that, however, I have come to realize that my obligation to parental honor involves essentially the willingness to try to reconcile in my own life conflicts between my parents which they themselves were never able to resolve. Since each of us is the child of two, always different, parents, this obligation would seem universal. God is interested in and partial to our liberation because the possibility of acquiring eventually wise hearts depends upon our erratic but ongoing progress toward maturity. For this reason I believe that only faith in God provides the basis for persistent pursuit of self-understanding.

It is a mistake to assume that we are natively capable of such a persistent search; this quest calls for more patience than most of us possess and requires us to face more unpleasantness about ourselves and more uncertainty about life than we might desire. As a result we begin to conceal, even from ourselves, facts or doubts which would be too upsetting to try to live with, and the process of self-discovery which began with such bravado often becomes just one more instance of progressive self-deception. Unfortunately organized religion is often an accomplice to such concealment.

The important fact for our present discussion, however, is this: the teens and twenties are the period of life in which we begin to learn what it means to make decisions and to live with their consequences. This is both an exciting and a disturbing experience. Is not the experience of choosing and living with our choices the very stuff of life? Our decisions need not always be right—probably they rarely are completely so—but it remains the case that something of the very essence of life is involved in the process of deciding. Nothing holds the potential for luring us more deeply into life and into ourselves than the choices we must make. In the area of decisions we are also required to become ever more knowledgeable about the realities of the world around us. We are limited in the capacity to choose wisely only by the scope and accuracy of our understanding of the environment and by the depth of our self-understanding. This is why both knowledge and self-knowledge are critically important for our lives and why God urges that we take the widest account of all of the considerations when we choose. We usually find it convenient to make decisions on the basis of something less than all of the factors. Considerations so neglected usually have their "say" at some later time, and often quite inconveniently.

It is not only exhilarating to be able to make decisions, it is also disturbing. To make a choice, for example, clearly means that one cannot know for certain all of the factors in a given situation, and therefore, one surely cannot know how a given set of events will work out. In all important decisions one is working with uncertainties; one cannot always be right. It would be more accurate to say that as a general rule one can be sure only of being partly wrong. However, the fact that one cannot choose flawlessly does not mean that decisions thereby become either unnecessary or impossible. The need for choice goes on, and having done the best we can, we must discover how we can live meaningfully with consequences which may have been quite unanticipated. This of course is the basis of the biblical assurance of justification by grace. We are not made right with God, anymore than we are made acceptable to our friends, on the basis of our flawlessness. We are reconciled to God by the assurance that there is nothing we can do which will be totally and permanently alienating; and in consequence of the realization that God calls us in love, we have the basis for doing the best we can with the decisions we must make.

Decisions are a central ingredient of our lives, and to withdraw from necessary decisions because of our fear of mistakes is more perilous than to err. The greater peril lies in the unrealizable yearning for a fault-free life. This is not to encourage error, but we must be able to affirm a world in which imperfect judgments are unavoidable. In view of this fact we need some basis for affirming our lives and attempting always to be responsible even when knowing that to be impossible. This is the point at which we may grasp, or be grasped by, God's persistent effort to call us into relationship. In the self-sacrificing love of Jesus Christ, the faulted person may see that there is nothing penitents may have done which God will not forgive. With such sight the believer recognizes also in Christ the human model to emulate for the sake of all humankind. Thus, as we realize that God endlessly calls us to our true vocation—to be as fully as possible ourselves as children of God—we discover the courage to make necessary decisions. Christ's example encourages us to an ever deeper understanding of ourselves and compassion for the world around us.

When we talk about a "relationship with God" we are not talking about something vague and "churchy" but a decisive reality with which Christianity is centrally concerned, something inseparable from the daily business of our lives. God is not a word which we pull out for special occasions, whether pious or impious; God is that gracious reality in whom the most important decisions may be made and lived with; through whom we are encouraged, even prodded, to deeper levels of self-understanding; within whom we know our destiny and the fate of all humankind. Faith in God is never merely assent to intellectual propositions. Instead, it is an act of trust that the humanity we see in Jesus is the humanity for which we were intended and that, as we aspire to it, there is nothing in this world that we need to fear. Neither is faith in God just a means of external identification—as when we say that somebody is a Methodist or Baptist or Roman Catholic. The absolute trust in

God's faithfulness liberates us from all of the lesser loyalties by which we are normally influenced, in order that we may act in this world consistently with that image of God which is in us. Our faith in God is the one bondage for which we were made; thus we are free to live humanely in the world with the men and women God has given us as neighbors.

Fundamentally, then, vocation has no reference to the work we do or should do in the world. Simply put, Christian vocation tells us to whom it is that we ultimately belong. In our faith we acknowledge our relationship with God, a relationship in which God is the giver and we the grateful recipients of the gift and by which we come to know our true humanity. To have a vocation, to know oneself called by God into relationship, is the means to true self-understanding: we are God's children, and each person is our neighbor. Embracing a Christian vocation means freedom from the fear of self-awareness and from the conventional bases upon which many people unthinkingly make most of their decisions.

It is neither accidental nor undesirable that old people constitute the majority population in churches. Those who regret this fact, who would prefer churches teeming with a younger population, are somewhat guilty of both a prejudice against the aging and a failure to appreciate why older people are there in greater numbers. The aging have distinctive things to accomplish in those later years, and in a society largely unsympathetic to the fact of age, churches and synagogues are among the few places where they can be free to pursue their tasks.

Is it true that we are confused and deceived about our ultimate identity? Is it true that we are often influenced in the decisions we make by factors of which we are only dimly aware or to which we can give only halfhearted approval? Is it true that we sense the importance of self-understanding but withdraw from it because of the demands which it clearly involves? Finally, is it true that we talk about human freedom and dignity but lack both an adequate basis for such attitudes and strong feelings for others? If you answer yes to any of these questions, then you may be at the point where you can comprehend the importance of a Christian vocation. In Jesus Christ we are called to a life of the deepest self-awareness, a life in which attitude and action have a high consistency, a life which willingly and joyfully acknowledges the neighbor as God's gift to us. This has been true from the beginning and throughout our lives, though we were often too preoccupied with realities which we assumed could substitute for such a calling. Aging is the last opportunity to acknowledge gladly that the call is for each one of us.

8

Images for Aging

During the months that I have been searching for images which might assist the aged to make something of their later years, I have had one recurring question. What evidence might help one identify the universal agenda for one's later years? There are two sources to which we must pay attention: people's actual experience and the Bible. For me, the endlessly intriguing and difficult task is to relate these two. It will not do to have two discrete sets of information. Each must provide questions and answers which illumine and deepen the other.

Some people are able to dismiss my question easily. Those appreciative of the great variety of human lives hold that there is no such agenda. Lives are too different, to say nothing of the varying individual and societal attitudes toward old age, to permit any such tasks for everybody. I have considerable sympathy with this attitude. At least superficially, individual people have quite different immediate tasks to address, from the grinding realities of being old and poor to the luxurious living of those who can afford expensive diversions. No two lives are quite identical.

At the other extreme are those who identify the inevitable fact of human mortality as the universal agenda of the aging. Clearly, it is impossible to argue with this brute reality, and it may well be that nothing is more important in aging than to come to terms with one's finitude. A time will come when each of us will only be remembered temporarily at best. An ancient Jewish writing makes quite clear that people have long realized the oblivion of death. Certainly, there are those whose worldly fame assures that they will not be immediately forgotten, but there are also many others:

> And there are some who have no memorial,
>   who have perished as though they had not lived;
> they have become as though they had not been born,
>   and so have their children after them. (Ecclesiasticus 44:9)

Only in the continuity of generations and the enduring blessing of their "righteous deeds" (v.10) is the sting of obliteration ameliorated. The sole justification of their nameless lives is the fact that "their descendants stand by the covenants. . . ." (v.12). In the last analysis covenant-faithfulness is the single enduring legacy. Beyond the reality of present life is its termination; nothing is more certain or potentially more unnerving than that. Perhaps this ultimate obscurity is the crucial clue to life's last and inescapable reality, of which all must learn to make some sense. I am inclined to assume this; certainly we lack firm information to the contrary. Not only may there be nothing more than that task, but we may need nothing more.

About this assertion I have misgivings. The emphasis too easily slides into the potentially morbid task of anticipating one's end. There is a power here of which we need to be keenly aware, but the task is to learn to use that power for more constructive life while time remains to us. The curse of the ancient Egyptian preoccupation with preparations for death was its indifference to the *quality of present life* for all people. That preoccupation provided the rationale for the enslavement of the worker populations to the grand projects of the pharaohs. Inordinate preoccupation with the future, especially that beyond death, also tends to denigrate present life and thereby diminishes the hope which empowers small, but meaningful, efforts to live more humanely today and tomorrow.

This sense of obligation to the present, this conviction that God can only be God for as long as we are able to be present to ourselves at all of life's stages, motivates my search for the agenda for all who grow old. How past recollections and a hoped-for future are reconciled in any individual life will reflect each person's inner self-understanding. The point, however, is that neither memory nor anticipation may control one's present. Writing in the early days of her eighth decade, May Sarton observes, "*I live more completely in the moment these days*, am not as anxious about the future, and am far more detached from the areas of pain, the loss of love, the struggle to get the work completed, the fear of death" (*At Seventy: A Journal*, 37 [italics added]). In every moment we have the exquisite and tormenting privilege to act as men and women made in the image of God. We are in varying degrees free *now* to be ourselves, with all our strengths and weaknesses. There will never be another time quite like this moment in which to be and to act as men and women so made. There may yet be many such opportunities, but none is as certain as the immediate present. It may also be true that each postponement makes it that much more difficult to claim the responsibility of one's inheritance as a child of God. Every delay tends to increase the reluctance to exercise one's God-given freedom, which is the essential ingredient of the image in which we are made. Without yet being able with certainty to identify aging's particular agenda, I am convinced that this privileged obligation is as true in one's last years as it was at any earlier time in life. At no prior time have we been quite the person we now are, nor will we again be exactly who we are today. Now is always and the only time to be present to oneself and to others.

The undeveloped recognition beneath this exhortation is that we are temperamentally unable to find satisfaction in the *limited* freedom we may be able to exercise. From society, from the media, and even from the churches we have been fed misleading attitudes about the amount of change of which we should be capable. Such inflated expectations cause us to undervalue, even to dishonor, the modest growth of which we are capable at any particular time. That this is all we are ever able to achieve, and never easily at that, is a precious truth which has been largely withheld from us. For this deprivation many pay an unwarrantedly heavy price.

A

The key to the search for an image adequate to the tasks of one's later years lies in the ancient Hebrew conviction that men and women are made in the image of God. Unlike the Greeks, with whose tradition the biblical religions have basically little in common, the Hebrews did not believe that people made God in their image. Exactly the opposite is affirmed: the creature's image is that of the Creator. The opening chapter of the first book of the Bible, the basis of both Jewish and Christian anthropology, asserts that human beings of all times and places are created in the image of God. Nothing is more basic than this conviction. It is the source of all human dignity; it informs the ways in which, under all circumstances, human beings are to deal with each other; it is the source of that freedom distinctive only to human life. From no human being—no matter age or circumstances—has that image been utterly removed. It may prove difficult, even impossible, at times to evoke, but that difficulty only demonstrates how far some lives are driven off course.

The last years of life represent the final chance to discover one's vocation as a person made in God's image. The major difficulties are twofold: to exercise one's God-given freedom and, relatedly, to undertake the work appropriate to one's age. Both of these challenges are formidable. There is deep inner resistance to using one's freedom, especially in those who have been rendered passive by societal pressures to conform and to undervalue the importance of modest change. No less problematic in this society is the fact that, as I have acknowledged, it is not easy to discover what may be aging's distinctive agenda.

As I write these words it seems that the two difficulties may be interrelated. The ability to exercise one's God-given freedom may depend upon some emerging recognition that there are distinctive and good things to be accomplished appropriately in one's later years. Freedom, which is distinctive to our humanity, is not arousable in a vacuum. It becomes possible only when real options are present *and* when one realizes that one's very being is at issue in the choice. As long as persons are in bondage to negative attitudes towards being old (which certainly is the case in America today), as long as aging people are urged to appear to be anything other than their age, there are no options which permit one to choose anything other than pretense. Given this restraint, one is not allowed gladly and defiantly to embrace one's old age for the God-given goodness inherent in it. But in a world in which God is central, it cannot be for nothing that we are allowed to grow old; certainly a life of pretense is no vocation for men and women made in God's image. Surely it cannot be the calling of those so made to pretend that they are other than they are. In pretense there is no basis for an identity commensurate with that image. This encouragement to pretense reveals society's deepest secularity: society itself creates the conditions whereby the aged may not be themselves and thus makes it impossible for God to be God for them. One is reminded of Jesus' harsh words to adversaries who "shut the kingdom of heaven against men; for you neither enter yourselves, nor allow those who would enter to go in" (Matt. 23:13). In combination with medicine's ability to extend lives we have created the perfect double bind: people are helped to live longer at the very time that they are forbidden to be their age. Under such circumstances there is little likelihood that aging men and women will exercise their freedom in pursuit of whatever may be their distinctive options.

The only hope is for a breakthrough in awareness of what these distinctive options for the aged may be. As older people become an ever larger percentage of the national population—a recent report estimates approximately forty million senior citizens by the year A.D. 2010 (*The Minneapolis Star and Tribune*, 3 October 1984)—the need to identify these options becomes imperative. Failure to do so assures that millions of old people will either trivialize themselves in costly pretenses or, where pretense is no longer possible, be resigned to empty, passive existence. Given the value we attach to productivity and action, this society may have trouble recognizing a creative potential for aging which it cannot honor. It is likely that even more of the aged will find themselves relegated to ghettos. Indeed, as the cost of maintaining such "useless" lives increases, society may generate a desire to be rid of the

burden. Despite their obvious importance, however, these possible societal consequences of our inability to assign positive value to growing
old are not the most urgent concern. Even the loveliest of retirement
centers will do little for those who cannot but dishonor their age. The
self-alienation of the aged is what merits immediate attention.

Two things concern me: the psychic and spiritual shape of a society
so truncated and the despair to which, by our attitudes, we consign
most old people. For them, in this society, it comes perilously close to
being for nothing that we grow older. The first of these concerns lies
beyond our present scope, and perhaps beyond my capability. It does
not seem to me conducive to long-range social health and well-being
for a sizable element to have, at best, second-class status. Ageism is, in
this regard, as damaging to the social fabric as is racism or sexism. As
an equalitarian and pluralistic nation we should recognize every person's need for meaningful contact with as wide a range of human life as
possible. Rarely acknowledged is what I take to be the deeper reason
for embracing such diversity: that *by acquaintance with the great variety of lives we have access to the great range of characters within ourselves.* The evil of sexism is not just what it does to women but what it
also keeps from happening in men. Sexist roles injure the social fabric
by treating women as inferiors but also make men's assent to potentials
within themselves impossible. Similarly those deprived of association
with old people remain alienated from the aged person latent within
each one of us. The generations, like the sexes and the races, need
more than tolerance for each other; they need to recognize that *for the
enlargement of their own humanity, each desperately needs the others.*
The interdependence of lives mandates that every person has something
to teach and to learn from all others. God willing, we shall all pass
through life's various stages. As we move towards an unfamiliar stage
such as aging we take courage both from our previous experience and
from those who are old. We recognize these sources of confidence because of continuities within and between us and all other human life.
This, of which we are often at best only dimly aware, cannot be over-
emphasized. It is bedrock for every person's journey through life's varied experiences.

Little progress in overcoming ageism is likely until we identify
those tasks to which older people should give themselves. In all socie-

ties the tasks will be difficult; they are especially difficult in one that is antipathetic to growing old. This antipathy has shaped the personal patterns and institutional life of the aged. It is highly unlikely that one will find in our society clues as to the vocation of old people made in the image of God. We need access to the lives of older people who have been less influenced by societal aversion to aging.

In order to gain such access to the lives of others, we must know what we are seeking. Simply stated, we are looking for guidance from the lives of people who are able to be their age. While our current focus is on older people, the reality we pursue is present over the entire course of all lives. Are people, or are they not, in touch with their own *actual* experience? Inasmuch as they have been so connected, they will become old people who affirm without despair the reality of their age. Aging *is* their present experience, with all its opportunities and pitfalls. Despite society's aversions, these will be men and women who value their age because that, and that only, is what they now have. Everything hinges on their ability to affirm that reality. There is no other basis on which God may become God for us than by our gradually becoming who we really are in aging.

B

Forty years ago I learned something from a great teacher, and I have never forgotten it. In a few seemingly unimportant words from James Muilenberg, I was given the key to identify the difficult but crucial task of one's later years and to understand the distinctiveness of the Bible: "In the year that King Uzziah died. . . ." These opening words of the sixth chapter of Isaiah present an example of the uniqueness of Jewish and Christian Scripture. Its importance for the central work of aging cannot be overstressed. Indeed, in the distinctive biblical understanding of the inextricable connection of one's experience in the world and one's awareness of God, we find the root of my insistence throughout this book that nothing more effectively discourages irenic aging than unfamiliarity with our experience. It has taken decades for me to grasp the full implications of what I learned at Union Theological Seminary, but that should not surprise me nor should it be cause for regret. There are some fundamental truths that reveal depths of meaning only as we bring even more experience to them. In fact, I increasingly suspect that there are some vital matters to be grasped *only* as we age. Having been mistaught to undervalue our actual experience, we are ill equipped to seek for the meaning of the final stage of life. By our endless preoccupation with the future—with plans and hopes that are legitimate *ingredients* of lives that reach both backwards and ahead—we have been as effectively cut off from present experience as were earlier generations whose preoccupation was exclusively with the past.

Let us return to that transforming experience of a young man in the temple at Jerusalem. Isaiah had often been to the temple before and may have admired or been awed by what he saw there. On a particular day, however, that place was the means of his radical encounter with God as King, the Lord of hosts. We have no reason to believe that, prior to that particular day, the young Isaiah was not a faithful Jew. As the child of a priestly family associated with the temple, he was probably appropriately instructed and was familiar with the community's worship. Undoubtedly, he was considered by others and by himself as a child of the ancient covenant.

What would not necessarily have been apparent to others, or even to himself, was the importance to him of King Uzziah. The king was, up to a point, one of Judah's great monarchs. The chronicles of leadership report that Uzziah, having ascended the throne as a young man, was by this time successful in all of the ways that would have impressed a youth. He had reigned for over fifty years; he was renowned as a warrior and administrator; "and his fame spread far, for he was marvelously helped, till he was strong" (2 Chron. 26:15). It requires little imagination to sense the importance to a boy of such a head of state. Whereas Scripture suggests that his achievements were the result of God's favor—"for he was marvelously helped"—it is neither difficult nor inappropriate to assume that Uzziah was like God for the child. The splendor of the court may well have been at least as impressive to a young person as was the awesomeness of the temple. Such mistaken identification is limited neither to youths nor to ancient times.

However, as the story tersely unfolds, "when [Uzziah] was strong he grew proud, to his destruction" (2 Chron. 26:16). In the temple Uzziah presumed authority to burn incense. True son of his ill-fated father, he felt that there was no limit to the exercise of his great power. In his anger at the priests' disapproval of his attempt to usurp their roles, he was afflicted with leprosy:

> And [the priests] thrust him out quickly, and he himself hastened to go out, because the LORD had smitten him. And King Uzziah was a leper to the day of his death, and being a leper dwelt in a separate house, for he was excluded from the house of the LORD. (2 Chronicles 26:20–21)

These are the immediate events of which Isaiah sought to make sense. He could not avoid the need to do so. His world had been shattered by the fate of the king, because he had over-invested in the meaning of that king's power. The disillusionment was undeniable. Something had to be done but it was not fully within his power to do it, for his identity had been snatched from him by the consequences of the unanticipated presumption of Uzziah. The question which experience made inescapable was simple and terrifying: who, then, is the king? Who can enable me to make sense of these events?

Not all people must struggle this hard to find meaning in their experience. There are alternatives with which we are all familiar. The more detached one is from what is actually happening in one's life, the less necessary the struggle: whether the onset of menstruation or of menopause, the sexual yearnings of adolescence or angina pains; whether something as painful as the loss of an anticipated promotion or as exquisite as reconciliation of a conflict. Many people unconsciously distance themselves from their experience in order to avoid distress. They do not want to deal with yesterday's frame of meaning, which today's experience threatens to destroy. Even when people are not so distanced, they may still find ways to obscure or to distort their actual experience. If an experience cannot be incorporated into an unchangeable frame of reference, we may begin to tell others, and finally ourselves, lies about it. I once had a colleague of some competence who could never admit that he had erred in any way. Such was his self-understanding, such the nature of his self-acceptance, that the admission of error was impossible. Pathetic mental gymnastics were often required to lodge the blame other than where it belonged. Later, when that person was continuing the pattern as somebody else's colleague, I was able to laugh about the behavior; but only much later did I realize sadly that his bondage should have made me cry.

Some people, like Isaiah, refuse to abandon their actual experience in favor of detachment or self-deception. For all such persons there is anguish. In fact, I am not being flippant when I suggest that our basic choice in life is about what kind of anguish we can affirm. Will it be that of progressive distancing from and deception about one's experience? Or, will it be the anguish of the endless adaptation of one's frame of meaning in order to be able to include in it, however awkwardly, today's events? One represents the refusal to grow, with all of the immediate comfort that entails; the other assents to the demands for growth with all of the immediate distress and long-range satisfactions it promises. God has set before us the ways of death and of life. If we are fortunate we will realize the choice and its implications early.

The choice between forms of anguish we are able to affirm may not be quite as simple as I suggest. We are all plagued by the conflict between the desire for deeper involvement in life and the reluctance to pay the unavoidable price of such growth. We have all pulled back from some of the challenges that have come to us over the decades, and one of the opportunities of aging is to help us recognize the cost of these instances. What matters in one's later years, however. is not these specific lost opportunities, but the general pattern of our earlier life: have we consistently avoided any serious change in our frame of meaning? Or have we, at least occasionally, been willing to struggle to modify our understanding of the world and of ourselves in it? If the former, then the likelihood of significant change of the pattern in one's late years is slight.

Few people escape having some traumatic experience that may determine their direction thereafter. Nevertheless, some people refuse the opportunity, often excruciatingly painful, inherent in the trauma. The young Isaiah was not such a one. Had he been, he would have been as unknown to us as myriad nameless ones who found a way "out." For Isaiah the issue of who or what warranted his trust would not disappear. Lacking a means of escape from the disorienting effects of King Uzziah's behavior and its consequences, unable to ignore his recent experience and its implications for his future, he was ready to realize the source of his true identity. No longer could he harbor illusions about the safety and well-being inherent in a powerful leader and a standing army. Gone were the self-understanding and national self-confidence grounded in "mighty men of valor . . . who could make war. . . to help the king against the enemy. . . engines, invented by skillful men . . . to shoot arrows and great stones" (2 Chron. 26:12–15). This was the undeniable disenchantment to which he had been brought, probably enhanced by awareness of the mounting territorial ambitions of the Assyrians who within his lifetime would subdue the neighboring and kindred nation of Israel. Isaiah's youthful trust had been misplaced.

Thus in the opening words of Isaiah 6, we have the clue to identify the crucial tasks of one's later years and also the distinctiveness of the biblical revelation. Both focus relentlessly on the importance of being in touch with one's actual experience. Isaiah did not just wander into the temple and have a "religious experience." On a biblical understanding of God and of human nature, that could not happen. It is not aimless people, those indifferent to their experience, who are made vividly aware of the divine presence and command. Such people have refused to be themselves as children of God as well as citizens of a society: they have declined both the anguish and the excitement of their true humanity. Therefore they have the modest and diminishing benefits of their detachment and deception. In their indifference to their experience, these are not biblical people. They are men and women who, never being evoked to change, will never hear the exquisite and awesome assurance which enveloped Isaiah in the temple:

> Holy, holy, holy is the LORD of hosts;
> the whole earth is full of his glory. (Isaiah 6:3)

The failure to affirm and to change is the tragic fate of many people long before they are aged.

Distinctive to the Bible is the insistence that God becomes God only as we become ourselves. Only as we claim for ourselves the brokenness, incompleteness, and infinite potential of our actual experience do the conditions exist for God to become a reality. As Psalm 73 and others remind us, there is no assurance that this will happen quickly. One of aging's possible wisdoms is to know that not even in painfully acknowledging our misery do we control God. God will not be coerced. Nevertheless, God will be present to us as we struggle to be ourselves. The revelation of God is inseparable from our willingness to be men and women rooted in all of the contingencies, disappointments, and yet glorious possibilities of human history. It is no accident that the anticipation of Jesus' birth should begin with the familiar words, "In those days a decree went out from Caesar Augustus that all the world should be enrolled" (Luke 2:1). The divine presence is revealed in no vacuum, to no aimless or detached person. Such disclosure is always and only to men and women intentionally involved in specific events in time and place. This insistence, distinctive to the Hebraic/Christian tradition, makes it imperative for us to lay claim to our own experience, preferably sooner but not later than in our last years.

While the imperative for this work may be the realization of one's aging, and while this is the immediate experience to be affirmed meaningfully, the fact of one's mortality is not the only reality which requires embracing. There is the vast experience of one's earlier life to be recalled and affirmed: all that mixed bag of achievements and failures, generosity and niggardliness, malice and inadvertence, loveliness and ugliness. We must accept all of the thoughtfulness and stupidity, the kindness and indifference that have caused us to become the old men and women we are now. While we are still alive there remain opportunities for additional generosity, appreciation, and—depending on our inventiveness—new departures. What we do for and with others will probably not be earth-shaking; however, one of aging's wisdoms is to realize that neither was anything we did earlier, despite the deceptions in which we engaged or tolerated from others. Few human behaviors are in themselves of enduring note, but deeds done with integrity and grace have a lasting impact. Works of love, perhaps especially the modest ones of which age remains capable, are transmitted from generation to generation. The flame of the divine presence is thus passed on.

Once again we turn to the words of the psalmist: "Lord, thou hast been our dwelling place in all generations" (Ps. 90:1). Whatever else the poet may have intended by his metaphor, it cannot exclude the recognition that in often unheralded works of love and justice, God has been persuasively present to all of the generations. Whether or not one will be capable of such God-revealing deeds at any stage of life depends upon the extent to which one is in touch with the varied experience of one's past and present. Given the ambivalent nature of all such experience, whether or not one acts as a life-giver or life-denier depends on one's knowing in whom or what we enduringly dwell.

C

Much earlier in this book I posed the question, "Is it for nothing that we grow older?" We may now answer the question simply. There is a twofold and belated agenda for the later years: to reacquaint ourselves with what, in fact, has been our gradually unfolding story and to embrace the reality that we have grown old and will die. These are imperatives not only in their own right but also for the sake of those with whom we shall live out our days. Future generations deserve the greatest integrity of which we are capable. In such truthful love of self and such generous love of our neighbor, we declare our love for that holy God in whom we belatedly realize we have always dwelt.

Because we have grown older we will not meet our tasks quite as we might have in earlier years. There *are* continuities between early and later life; the elements which were present from the outset do not disappear. But the empowering configurations change between youth and age. We do not, for example, necessarily lose the sexual energy which was so imperious in adolescence and early adulthood and which remained an important dimension of the adult decades. However, though I would not denigrate this beautiful gift, the fact is that in time it loses some of its commanding power. Something similar may be said for the ubiquitous drive to succeed. In time we also lose some of our preoccupation with other people's judgments of us; we recognize the unavoidable inaccuracy and fundamental irrelevance of such opinions. Increasingly we are able to assign such views less importance than ever was possible earlier.

As we grow older, we are more and more able to be just who we are. We know that most things could not have been other that they were, and we are willing to live with their consequences. Although this outlook sounds dangerously close to resignation, I see no way to avoid that proximity. That very realization seems intrinsic to aging's agenda. To the end of life there remains the possibility of change, even if the changes will be minor ones. One seemingly minor change, however, makes all the difference in the world: the ability to affirm those realities which one discovers about one's self.

D

Throughout this book we have inquired about the possible ingredients of the wise heart for which the psalmist prayed. We have proceeded on the assumption that there are some things to learn for which the aged may be best fitted. Chronological age does not necessarily make one teachable; at all of life's stages all people are potentially learners. The problem is that the responsibilities of one's earlier decades often unavoidably divert one's attention to other matters. The psalmist's hunch is that, if one can but rightly pay attention, there is *something in experience which is instructive*, something to which our ordinary preoccupations effectively blind us. The psalmist asks that we might be taught "to number our days that we may get a heart of wisdom." Note that the request is not asking for information about the length of life. He knows both that this varies with individuals and that ultimately the literal number of our days is not the issue. Rather, he prays for the wisdom inherent in the realization that one's days are numbered. We do not live forever.

Thus, the prayer is that we may know our mortality, for we will live differently once that is grasped. We ask God to teach us to live towards our inescapable deaths, in order that we may learn wisely to live as children of God. On this understanding of our identity, which is absolutely central to the biblical faith and largely obscured by so much of contemporary life, we are beginning to apply our hearts to wisdom. However else we may at earlier times have understood ourselves and been understood by others, however adequate these ways of self-presentation seemed, they must yield to the deeper understanding of ourselves as God's mortal creatures. Futhermore, it is not just intellectual knowledge the psalmist desires but a new learning by which the heart is made wise. Our need is not only to know the predictable number of days and years left to us but to realize that our time is finite. This wisdom gives us a new way of looking at everything, including our own past. In this light we have eyes to see and ears to hear the wonderful sights and sounds which, one day, our senses will no longer receive.

To acknowledge this is not a matter of optimism or pessimism; it is bedrock reality. Gladly affirming this wisdom will make all the difference in the world.

This is aging's new direction, the new learning for which we need adequate imagery. From the empowering clarity of aging's viewpoint, having access to all that has been and realizing what lies ahead, we are able to embrace our story gracefully rather than with shame or self-disgust. The actions that we have regretted, the innumerable opportunities that we have missed, the many times that we have needed forgiveness are only part of what has been our life. There have also been those "golden flecks," often hardly noticed at the time, to enrich our final acceptance of ourselves as God's own.

Unavoidably, life is different towards the end. It could not be otherwise, despite the continuities. It is as though within our own life span many generations within us have searched for wise hearts, and all have found this wisdom in the realization that historically, currently, and perpetually, we dwell in God. That knowledge proves sufficient even, or perhaps especially, in old age.